the next level

the oaks edition

a 31-day journey

scott wilson

with patrick springle
foreword by dr. samuel r. chand

the next level

a message of hope for hard times

Formatting and jacket design by Anne McLaughlin, Blue Lake Design, Dickinson, Texas
Published in the United States by Baxter Press, Friendswood, Texas

ISBN: 978-1-888237-89-4

WHAT PEOPLE ARE SAYING ABOUT *THE NEXT LEVEL*

"Take a look into scriptures to find that true faith is built upon life's hard lessons. In *The Next Level,* Scott Wilson takes you on a journey of self-discovery, a look at how hard times in life can be the tool that God uses to propel you to the next level of faith, love, and intimacy with your Lord."
—Shane Everett of Shane and Shane, recording artists

"For the past several years, Scott Wilson has been my pastor, leadership mentor, and friend. His passion and effectiveness for developing people to fulfill their destiny is extraordinary. This book will change your circumstances because it will change you."
—Steve Wilson, Founder/Owner of Texzon Electric

"Whether you're a businessman, lawyer, professor or politician, you need this book. Scott Wilson captures inspirational insight that will change your thought process and guide you through the tests that come on the road to spiritual growth. Get ready to dig deep."
—Hon. Chris Parvin, Esq., lawyer and city councilman

"*The Next Level* is an incredible book. It's an amazing tool to help people understand God's purposes for the struggles they face!"
—John Houston, President, J Houston Homes, LLC

"In his book, Pastor Scott Wilson brings a 21st century perspective to apply biblical truth to the challenges facing all of us. Many well-known characters and stories from the Bible receive a fresh interpretation to illustrate the seasons of testing in our lives. If you want to make those seasons productive so you pass your tests, this book can give you hope and handles on the hardest problems you face. I highly recommend that you too reach for *The Next Level.*"
—Tom Davis, attorney

THE OAKS FELLOWSHIP

Have you ever found yourself in a situation that looked hopeless or seemed destined to fail? One in which you feel overwhelmed by fear, uncertainty and hurt? We understand. We've been there too.

Sometimes, answers come in a flash, but quite often, it takes a while to uncover them—but in that moment, everything changes. Have you ever experienced a moment when hurts are healed, fears are relieved, and anger subsides? In those moments God whispers, "I'm here, and I care about you very much." These moments give us faith . . . and our faith drives us.

At The Oaks, we believe that God has called us to live in the world of the impossible. Through listening to his voice and staying connected to his Spirit, we've seen the impossible become reality in countless lives.

God always has something unbelievable up his sleeve: the unexpected . . . just what's needed . . . right when it's needed. That's why we turn to him when we face problems that seem impossible.

The apostle Paul wrote in one of his letters: "God can do anything, you know—far more than you could ever imagine or guess or request in

your wildest dreams! He does it not by pushing us around but by working within us, his Spirit deeply and gently within us" (Ephesians 3:20-21 *The Message*).

At The Oaks Fellowship, we're a group of people who join together to worship God and to experience relevant, compelling and creative life-changing messages based on truths from God's word—the Bible. We're excited about sharing the love of Christ by caring for each other and our communities.

We'd be honored to have you join us at any of our weekly services. To find out more about The Oaks Fellowship and a campus near you, go to www.theoaksonline.org, call 214.376.8208 or email us at info@theoaksonline.org.

I would like to dedicate this book to my beautiful wife Jenni. There is no one in the world like her. She is the best friend I've ever had. She is the most dedicated mother I've ever seen, and the greatest source of encouragement and wisdom in my life. Thank you, Jenni, for everything you do. I love you.

—Scott

CONTENTS

ACKNOWLEDGEMENTS

First, I want to thank The Oaks Fellowship family. You are the best. I appreciate the elders of the church for their support in the vision for this book and the community-wide campaign. Thank you for dreaming big with me.

I'd also like to thank my teaching team—Dan Call, Chris Railey, and Paul Hurckman—for their input, and Justin Lathrop for all the work and encouragement he has been to me in promoting this project.

I'd like to recognize my friend and writer, Pat Springle, who helped get this book out of my heart and down on paper. Your contribution to this book has been phenomenal. You are a true gift from God. Thank you for all your diligent work and guidance. You are amazing.

Finally, I would like to thank my wife Jenni and my three boys—Dillon, Hunter, and Dakota—you are the greatest joy of my life. Thank you for letting me share your stories with the world. I owe you!

FOREWORD

When we experience difficulties—from minor inconveniences like getting stuck in a slow lane of traffic to major calamities such as disease, betrayal, or a wayward child—they shake the foundations of our lives. Our culture tries to convince us that everything should be fun, easy, and quick. Problems, we're sure, just don't belong in our lives at all, and when they occur, we want them to be gone as soon as possible. But I've found that the most important lessons I've ever learned have come through the most difficult times in my life. I didn't enjoy them, and I wouldn't want to go through them again, but I wouldn't trade those lessons for anything.

When we encounter roadblocks and heartaches, our natural, spontaneous response is to ask questions such as, "Why me?" "God, what are you doing? I don't deserve this." "God, where are you? Don't you even care?" I'm not going to tell you that those questions are wrong and that you shouldn't ask them. In fact, those who ask such questions are in good company. The psalms in the Bible are full of heartfelt expressions of dismay and disappointment, and even anger toward God. But I'm convinced that God delights in us engaging him, even in our doubts about his goodness and presence. As long as we are asking him questions, we're pursuing him, and sooner or later, we'll find an answer.

God's answer to our questions, though, may not address the "whys" we've been asking. His answers are most often "who," not "why" or "how" or "when." Job endured the most tragic circumstances any person ever faced. He lost his family, his home, his livelihood, and his health. All he had left was a nagging wife! Naturally, he asked God many questions, and finally, God showed up to answer. In one of the longest monologues by God in the Bible, he demonstrated his love, wisdom, and power in unmistakable ways to Job. After God finished speaking, Job realized that God knows what he's doing, he cares deeply, and he can be trusted. God, the ultimate "who," is supremely trustworthy. That was enough of an answer for Job.

This book is a beautiful and compelling account of people in the Bible, including men and women who trusted God in their darkest moments, and those who gave up on God when they needed him most. In these stories, we don't get any sugarcoated saints. These were real people who faced the same kinds of difficulties you and I face when we struggle with life. Some trusted God; some didn't. But we learn just as much from those who failed (perhaps because we can identify with them) as those who thrived in hard times.

The Next Level is designed to give us a fresh, hopeful, faith-filled perspective about the struggles we face. Trusting God in the middle of difficulties is one of the most challenging elements of the walk of faith, but when we find him there, God strengthens our faith and deepens our love for him. We all face tests. This book helps us learn from these experiences instead of being crushed by them. I trust God will use the stories, insights, and reflections in each chapter to inspire you. You'll find him to be supremely trustworthy—even in the darkest moments of your life.

Dr. Samuel R. Chand
Consultant, "dream releaser," and author of nine books, including
Who's Holding Your Ladder?

www.samchand.com

INTRODUCTION: EMBRACING GOD'S TESTS

In my years as a follower of Christ and a pastor, I've noticed that a few central truths have dramatic effects on a person's spiritual vitality — and none of these is more important than the truth that God has good and specific purposes for the tests he gives us. Our perceptions about the difficulties we face (unique or repetitive, cataclysmic or seemingly insignificant) shape our responses to these difficulties, and they also have a profound impact on our attitudes, our relationships, and even our physical health.

When I experience a struggle in my life, sometimes I see it as a prison, and sometimes as a classroom. If I see it as a prison, my only thought is to escape the pain and confusion as quickly as possible (and maybe defend my innocence to anyone who might judge me). But at other times, I look through a different lens at these problems, and I see that they are classrooms where God teaches me life's most valuable lessons. The difference in perspective determines my outlook and my response. If I see my struggles as a classroom, I don't resent the problems and the people who caused them. In fact, I open my heart to God and invite him to fill me with wisdom, grace, and courage as I face these difficulties.

God has a wonderful purpose for each of us. Paul wrote to the believers in Ephesus that God has specifically created and crafted us to fulfill crucial roles in his kingdom. He told them, "For we are God's workmanship, created in Christ Jesus to do good works, which God prepared in advance for us to do" (Ephesians 2:10). All of us, though, need training in knowledge and skills to prepare us to serve effectively. The class for this training is in session every moment of every day, but like any competent school, tests are the crucial moments where we find out if we've made progress or if we still have more to learn.

Some of the tests we face are major turning points, but most of the ones we face each day are more like pop quizzes. In fact, if we aren't observant, we may not even notice them. Our tests may have the menacing face of someone like Egypt's pharaoh who gets in the way of what God has called us to do, but God's exams almost always reveal the content of our hearts. Waiting is a common (and excruciating) test to see if we'll keep trusting God during difficult delays. Throughout the Bible, we find men and women who faced challenges. Some of their problems were caused by evil people, some by unseen circumstances, some by their own foolish choices, and some were engineered by God himself. Joseph endured slavery because his brothers hated him, and he was thrown into an Egyptian dungeon because his master's wife lied about him. He hadn't done anything wrong, but God had a sweeping purpose to use his suffering to rescue his family and the Jewish nation. Job's difficulties began with the cataclysmic loss of almost everything dear to him, but his pain multiplied because of his wife's hopeless anger and friends who blamed him for his troubles. Jesus certainly wasn't immune to difficulties. In fact, he endured far more heartache, ridicule, and suffering than anyone in history. In the garden before he was arrested, he came almost to the breaking point—but he didn't break. Jesus, though, was never surprised by the trouble he faced. He fully understood that it was part of living in this world. We can have the same perspective.

When we feel out of control, we don't have to be resigned to despair. Far from it. If we realize that God will use every struggle, every pain, and every moment of confusion to teach us how to live, we'll embrace our trials instead of despising them. Paul made this point in his letter to the Christians in Rome. He had experienced all kinds of persecution and privation, but he was thoroughly convinced that God would use every difficulty for good purposes in his life. In the crucible of struggles and confusion, he concluded that suffering is God's classroom. He wrote:

> "We also rejoice in our sufferings, because we know that suffering produces perseverance; perseverance, character; and character, hope. And hope does not disappoint us, because God has poured out his love into our hearts by the Holy Spirit, whom he has given us" (Romans 5:3-5).

Another translation says that we "exult" in our tribulations. Exult means *to take delight in*. Is that possible? (Is it even sane?) Yes, but we don't take great delight in the suffering itself. Instead, we delight that suffering causes us to draw closer to God and produces godly character qualities in us. That's Paul's clear conviction.

The tests we face reveal what's really in our hearts. We're like sponges. When difficulties squeeze us, the actual content of our hearts comes pouring out. In those moments of self-revelation, we come face to face with the truth about our spiritual condition. Sometimes what comes out is faith, hope, and love, but too often, it's resentment, despair, and a penchant for blaming others. God loves us, but he's much more committed to developing our character than protecting our comfort. Allowing us to be squeezed from time to time gives us opportunities to make corrections in our attitudes and actions.

How do you respond to setbacks in your life? If you're like most people, you may:

- Quickly blame someone else, even if you were part (or all) of the cause.

- Try to run away from the pain and the responsibility.

- Feel resentful toward people who hurt you and those who failed to help you, and toward God for letting it happen.

- Believe that you deserve better and you shouldn't have to endure suffering like that.

- Try to "medicate" the pain by using alcohol, drugs, pornography, shopping, food, or some other behavior or substance.

- Conclude that life isn't fair, and it's not worth it to even try.

I believe that much of the confusion, passivity, and resentment in Christians today come from a misinterpretation of struggles in their lives. They have listened to all the messages in our culture that promise a worry-free life, popularity, and riches if we just buy this product or that service. Suffering, they've concluded, isn't part of God's plan — well, maybe it is for you, but certainly not for me!

But it is. God gives us many wonderful blessings: spiritually, financially, relationally, and physically, but we live in a fallen world with flawed people like us. We simply can't escape struggles and heartaches, but we can learn to respond to them with clear-eyed faith. We desperately need to see God's purpose in every circumstance in our lives. In his book *Reaching for the Invisible God*, Philip Yancey recounts, "Gregory of Nicea once called St. Basil's faith 'ambidextrous' because he welcomed pleasures with the right hand and afflictions with the left, convinced both would serve God's design for him."[1] When we have more insight about God's purposes for our pain, we gain "ambidextrous faith," trusting him in the good times and the bad to teach us valuable lessons and shape us into the image of Christ.

Do you remember the very best teacher you ever had? I sure do. It wasn't the easiest course, but I learned the most. My teacher had good intentions: to teach us so that the lessons changed our lives. His passionate demeanor and the challenges he gave us inspired us to learn. He gave the hardest tests I ever had in school, but in that environment, I never

---

1   Philip Yancey, *Reaching for the Invisible God*, (Zondervan, Grand Rapids, Michigan, 2000), p. 69.

resented them. And he always rewarded students who excelled. I went to class each day eager to dive into the lecture and the discussions. My experience with that teacher is a model of the way God wants you and me to learn from him. His intentions are always for our good—never to hurt us—but his tests are difficult. If we understand his heart, we'll rise to the challenges and trust him to instruct and inspire us. We'll see every test as a steppingstone of growth, and he'll reward us every step of the way.

When we pass our tests (either the first time we face them or eventually after many attempts), we're able to teach and model those lessons for those around us, especially for our children. And we can be sure: They're watching! If we have an accurate understanding about the value of tests, we'll welcome them instead of resenting them. In fact, we'll cry out for God to examine us so that we can reach our full potential. King David had that perspective. He prayed,

- "Examine me, O Lord, and try me;
    test my mind and heart" (Psalm 26:2).

- "Though you probe my heart and examine me at night,
    though you test me, you will find nothing;
    I have resolved that my mouth will not sin" (Psalm 17:3).

- "Search me, O God, and know my heart;
    Test me and know my anxious thoughts.
  See if there is any offensive way in me,
    And lead me in the way everlasting" (Psalm 139:23-24).

Paul encouraged the Corinthians to take a good look at their lives and be honest about their walks with God. He wrote, "Test yourself to see if you are in the faith; examine yourselves!" (2 Corinthians 13:5)

James penned perhaps the most familiar passage about the benefits of facing tests. He wrote, "Consider it pure joy, my brothers, whenever you face trials of many kinds, because you know that the testing of your faith develops perseverance. Perseverance must finish its work so that you may be mature and complete, not lacking anything" (James 1:2-4). Do you want to be mature and complete, not lacking in anything? The path of growth is paved with tests. If we want what God wants, we can't escape his curriculum of testing. And in fact, like David, we'll embrace every test that comes our way.

The truth about testing includes these important principles:

1. We all experience tests at each stage of our growth. God tailors his curriculum to fit our maturity and our needs at each point in our spiritual lives. They aren't the same for each of us — God is much too creative for that. But we can be sure that all along the way, we'll face tests that appropriately challenge us and stimulate us to trust God more deeply than ever.

2. Our goal is to pass every test. When we see tests as beneficial, we won't resent them and we won't run from them. We'll pray, "Lord, I'm yours. Teach me from this experience." We'll listen intently to his Spirit, and as we face the difficulty, we'll learn to trust him even more.

3. God won't give us more than we can handle. Sometimes, the tests can take us to the breaking point, but Paul assures us that God won't push us over the brink. He assured the Corinthians, "No temptation has seized you except what is common to man. And God is faithful; he will not let you be tempted beyond what you can bear. But when you are tempted, he will also provide a way out so that you can stand up under it" (1 Corinthians 10:13). That's God's clear promise.

4. Self-protection and human popularity can't compete with divine promotion. When we feel threatened, our normal human response is to defend ourselves, blame others, and try to win approval so we feel better again. In God's school, though, he has a different lesson for us to learn. He wants us to first and foremost seek him. We'll probably have to change our old methods of dealing with our struggles. Peter encouraged us, "Humble yourselves, therefore, under God's mighty hand, that he may lift you up in due time. Cast all your anxiety on

him because he cares for you" (1 Peter 5:6-7). In times of testing, look to God for wisdom, and when the time is right, you can be sure he'll reward your faith in the midst of struggle.

My dad always had a way to communicate biblical truth to his sons. I remember him telling us, "Boys, you better put on the belt of truth, or you're gonna lose your britches. That could be pretty humiliating!" He was teaching us that if we didn't learn to receive and accept truth, we would only be hurting ourselves and eventually hindering the work God wants to do in our lives. Understanding God's design to use testing in our lives is an important part of the belt of truth God wants us to wear.

Do you see God as a teacher who gives tests designed to sharpen your mind, fill your heart, and equip you with skills? Or do you see every difficulty as a prison you need to run from? In this 31-day journey, we'll look at people in the Bible and how they faced tests. Some of them passed with flying colors, and some failed miserably. The Scriptures tell us about them so that we'll pay attention and learn from their examples. The tests they faced aren't very different from the ones you and I face today. Though we sometimes feel that we're the only ones wrestling with a problem, we're not alone in our struggles. The "great cloud of witnesses" in heaven is cheering us on, and there are people around us who understand, care, and are more than willing to lend a helping hand.

All of us face tests every day—large or small, obvious or hidden. Our response to these difficulties is a window into the condition of our hearts. Author and speaker John Maxwell identified three distinct conditions revealed by our response to tests:

- **Inward Poverty:** When we face problems, we become angry or frustrated, and we instinctively blame others for our difficulties. We try to escape the problem as quickly as possible. Our response shows that we've failed to accept God's supremacy, our role as stewards, and God's promises and provisions for our lives.

- **Inward Plateau:** The tests reveal that we are stuck in a spiritual rut.

We've grown in the past, but we're not making progress now. In this stage, we often become resentful and judgmental of others who are doing well.

- **Inward Progress:** We trust that God is at work even in the middle of our struggles. We don't demand immediate relief, and we don't insist that God tell us how he's using the difficulties we face. Even in times of confusion and darkness, knowing that he's good, wise, and strong is enough to give us confidence in the ultimate outcome. Our faith-filled response to tests demonstrates that we've learned important lessons and have put them into practice in our lives.[2]

On each page of this book, I hope God gives you a sense of "inward progress" as you take steps to trust him and move to the next level in your walk of faith. As you read each chapter, ask God to open your heart to help you see him as the ultimate Teacher whose tests are designed to build you up, not to tear you down. Trust him to soften your heart and make you receptive to his leading and his wisdom. As you read and work through the exercises each day, I trust you'll develop "two-handed faith," trusting God in the good times and in the difficulties, assured that he will use both for good in your life "so that you may be mature and complete, not lacking anything."

For a video blog by Pastor Scott for each day of this journey, go to www.journeytothenextlevel.com. You can also post prayer requests and praise reports about each day's lesson.

---

2   Adapted from *The Leadership Test* by John Maxwell, www.iequip.org

Adam and Eve
THE OWNERSHIP TEST

"You will not surely die," the serpent said to the woman. "For God knows that when you eat of it your eyes will be opened, and you will be like God, knowing good and evil." When the woman saw that the fruit of the tree was good for food and pleasing to the eye, and also desirable for gaining wisdom, she took some and ate it. She also gave some to her husband, who was with her, and he ate it. (Genesis 3:4-6)

One day when I was a boy, my dad took my brothers and me to Mc-Donald's for lunch. He loaded up a tray with burgers, fries, and drinks, and we sat at a table for a feast every child loves. Dad was, as I recall, on one of his diets, so he didn't order any fries for himself. That day in the middle of all the commotion of lunch with four little boys, Dad reached over and took two French fries from my brother Bracy's bag. Bracy looked up at him with a shocked look on his face and said, "Hey, what are you doing? Dad, those are my fries! If you want some, go buy your own."

Dad took a few seconds to digest his son's insolence. He came to the conclusion that this would be one of his infamous "teaching moments." Suddenly, his voice boomed out for everyone in the restaurant to hear, "Son, I bought those fries for you. In fact, I bought everything you own.

If I wanted to buy you 20 more orders of fries, I could do that. If I chose to never buy you another bag of fries for the rest of your life, I could do that, too." He paused for a second to let his words sink in. (I'm not sure, but I think the lady standing at the fryer was nodding at this point.) Then he brought it home: "Son, you've lost perspective on who I am and who you are. I'm your father, and I give you everything you have. Remember that, son, and it'll change how you view your possessions for the rest of your life." He made his point—to Bracy, to me, and to everybody else within earshot.

For the first people on earth, as well as for us, everything we enjoy is a gift from God. He is the Creator. He simply spoke a word and the entire universe was flung into the skies. Astronomers tell us that the universe is almost 14 billion light-years across, and each light-year is six billion miles. The scope is literally unimaginable! When I put one of the kid's toys together at Christmas, I think I'm pretty special. Compared to God's creation, man's efforts, even our most astounding technological inventions, are just a breath in the hurricane of God's creative energy. God's power and his initiative in creating the universe give him a distinct position as the owner of all. Even our ability to earn a salary is a gift from God. When we grasp this fact, we understand that we are simply his stewards of a small patch of his vast creation. And when we forget that he is the Creator and owner of all, we get into big trouble. Just ask Adam and Eve.

The first couple had it made. They enjoyed fantastic weather, delicious food, the best sex, intimate encounters with God, and the highest purpose people can experience. God had given them dominion over everything their eyes could see. They needed absolutely nothing and delighted in everything, but somehow it wasn't enough. The serpent whispered in Eve's ear to question God's authority, and she listened. What was his lure? He told her that if she ate of the forbidden tree, "You will not surely die. For God knows that when you eat of it your eyes will be opened, and you will be like God, knowing good and evil" (Genesis 3:4-5).

The essence of the serpent's deception was that Eve could turn her relationship with God upside down. She didn't have to be submissive to him; she could be "like God." What in the world does that mean? It means she would be autonomous, free from all constraints, and not responsible to him for her choices. Instead of being the steward of all God created, she wanted to be the owner. The temptation proved too strong for her, and she ate the forbidden fruit. (We may get upset with Eve for being deceived by the serpent, but Adam doesn't have an excuse. He ate it knowingly and willingly. Bad choice, Adam.)

From that day to this, our human nature has tried to overturn the order of creation. We want to be the owners, in charge and on top. From time to time, God breaks in and speaks to us like my father talked to Bracy to remind us that he's the Creator and owner of everything, but we are slow learners. Every moment of every day, we face the ownership test. When we get our paycheck, do we cling to it and feel proud that we've earned it on our own, or do we stop to thank God that he gave us the ability to earn a living for us and our families? When we struggle through difficult financial times, do we worry and fret, or do we trust that God, our gracious Father who "owns the cattle on a thousand hills" will provide for us in his way and in his timing? When was the last time you walked around your house, looked at every piece of furniture, every dish and pot, and every piece of jewelry and said, "God, it's all yours. Thank you for letting me have it for a while, but it's yours to do with as you see fit."

A friend of mine lives on the Gulf Coast. A couple of years ago, Hurricane Rita barreled toward his community. He and a friend put plywood over the windows of their homes as their families evacuated with the few valuables they could pack in their cars. Then, the day before landfall, the storm grew to a Category 5 monster headed straight for him. Before he walked out of the boarded up house, my friend walked through each room looking at all the antiques, family heirlooms, furniture he and his wife had bought during their marriage, paintings, and other valuables that had to be left behind. As he walked around, he prayed, "Lord, all this is yours. There may not be a stick left when I come back, but I put it all in your hands. Do with it as you please." Just before the hurricane hit the coast, it shifted east and spared his community, but he said that this experience helped him let go of things he had cherished too much for too long.

The heart of the difference between ownership and stewardship is our concept of God. Author and professor J. I. Packer observes,

"Today, vast stress is laid on the thought that God is personal, but this truth is so stated as to leave the impression that God is a person of the same sort we are —weak, inadequate, ineffective, a little pathetic. But this is not the God of the Bible! Our personal life is a finite thing: it is limited in every direction, in space, in time, in knowledge, in power. But God is not so limited. He is eternal, infinite, and almighty. He has us in His hands; but we never have Him in ours. Like us, He is personal, but unlike us He is great. In all its constant stress on the reality of God's personal concern for His people, and on the gentleness, tenderness, sympathy, patience, and yearning compassion that He shows towards them, the Bible never lets us lose sight of His majesty, and His unlimited dominion over all His creatures."[3]

If we see ourselves as equal with God (or even a little wiser about what we need) with the right to direct our lives and as owners of everything around us, we will demand our own way and resist God's authority over us. When our purpose is comfort and affluence, we want to possess as much as possible to make us happy and look prosperous in the eyes of others. But the things around us aren't ours, and we don't even own ourselves. God does. Paul wrote the Corinthians, "Do you not know that your body is a temple of the Holy Spirit, who is in you, whom you

---

3   J. I. Packer, *Knowing God*, (Intervarsity Press, Downers' Grove, Illinois, 1973), p. 74.

have received from God? You are not your own; you were bought at a price. Therefore honor God with your body" (1 Corinthians 6:19-20).

The first test for Adam and Eve was about ownership, and the fundamental test for us is the same one: Do we see ourselves as the center of the universe, or are we fully, completely, wholeheartedly God's, enjoying immense privileges as his children, but with the responsibility to represent him all day every day? Is life about our comfort, our excitement, and our pleasure, or is it about honoring the one who created us, redeemed us, and has given us the opportunity to join him in touching people's lives?

The answers to these questions shape every other choice we make, but the temptation to be first, the possessor, and on top is very strong. Every day, in one way or another, I wake up and say to God, "Lord, I'm yours today. I don't know what I'll face today, but you're in charge. I'll follow you wherever you lead, say whatever you want me to say, and do whatever you want me to do." No matter what comes, I trust God will use successes to expand his fame, and he'll use struggles to shape my life so that I seek him more. If I have this attitude, he can shape me a little more into the person he wants me to be.

If we see ourselves as owners, we have to either figure out how to make life work on our own, or worse, we try to manipulate God to give us more comfort, pleasure, and excitement. God, though, doesn't play that game. In fact, he is at cross-purposes with us when we try to use him for selfish gain. If we insist on being like God, demanding to be autonomous and the owner of everything in our lives, we'll suffer spiritual bankruptcy and emotional stress. God created us to be grateful children, not demanding owners. When our attitudes are right, we experience the joy of his presence and peace. When we enjoy prosperity, we humbly acknowledge, "God, you gave this to me, and I want to use it to honor you." And when we suffer financial reversals, relational struggles, or sickness, we respond, "Lord, I belong to you, and I want to please you in sickness or in health, when things go well and when they don't."

The ownership test is the first one recorded in Scripture, and it is one of the most common tests we face. In many ways, knowing *who we are* and *whose we are* is at the heart of every other test in our lives.

If we begin to truly understand that God is in control of everything, owns everything and gives to us wisely and generously, how does this help us in our day-to-day tests?

What are some possessions, positions, or abilities you've owned that you need to turn over to God so that you become his faithful steward? What has kept you from turning these things over? What do you need to do to fully turn them over?

What difference will turning these areas over to God make in your attitude, peace of mind, and generosity?

God, you are the Creator and owner of everything. Help me to . . .

Cain and Abel
THE COMPARISON TEST

Then the Lord said to Cain, "Why are you angry? Why is your face downcast? If you do what is right, will you not be accepted? But if you do not do what is right, sin is crouching at your door; it desires to have you, but you must master it." (Genesis 4:6-7)

It didn't take long for sin to take root in human nature and poison relationships. Just after we see Adam and Eve failing the first test, we find one of their sons failing another one. As a reminder of his forgiveness, God instructed the first family to offer sacrifices to him. At each of these events, they'd remember that God is the owner of everything and they desperately need his forgiveness. God didn't leave them wandering alone in the wilderness outside Eden. His directive to offer sacrifices was part of his plan to keep them close to him. The sons, Cain and Abel, understood the importance of these sacrifices.

Abel was a rancher, and he brought the best animal in his flock to offer to God. God was very happy with Abel's sacrifice. Cain was a farmer, and he brought fruit and grain to offer to God. For some reason, God wasn't thrilled with Cain's offering. Later in the Scriptures, we read that sin offerings always involved the death of an animal. Perhaps God had instructed both men to offer animals and Cain disobeyed, or maybe Cain made his offering halfheartedly or grudgingly. Or perhaps Cain's offering wasn't the "firstfruits" of his harvest. The passage tells us that Cain brought his offering "in the course of time," but Abel brought "fat portions from some of the firstborn of his flock." Whatever the reason, God didn't accept his sacrifice.

When Cain found that he failed the test, he had a couple of options. He could have said, "God, I want to do it right next time. Thanks for giving me another chance." But that's not how he responded. The Scriptures tell us that he "was very angry, and his face was downcast."

God noticed his anger, and he warned Cain, "If you do what is right, will you not be accepted? But if you do not do what is right, sin is crouching at your door; it desires to have you, but you must master it" (Genesis 4:7). God was giving him a second chance! But Cain looked at his brother and despised the fact that God approved of him. He asked Abel to meet him out in a field, and there, Cain killed his brother.

One of the lessons we learn from Cain and Abel is that comparison kills. It robs us of peace, destroys our sense of sanity, and poisons relationships. We become so consumed with anger at those who seem to prosper more than us that we blame them for our own sins. It's human nature — sinful human nature — to size up our status in relation to those around us. We compare our houses, cars, beauty, vacations, bonuses, hair, noses, prestige, and every conceivable thing in life to see where we are in the pecking order. If we're above this person, we can feel good for a while. But if that person climbs a bit higher or buys something that people ooh and aah about, we secretly (or not so secretly) resent it.

In his insightful book, *The Call,* author Os Guinness observes that people compare themselves to others with the same strengths. For instance, a concert pianist compares her skills and acclaim to other renowned pianists, not bank presidents. And star basketball players compare their skills and salaries to others in their sport, not authors. We may not all play on the same field as we compare ourselves with others, but it's woven deep into the fabric of our natures to compare ourselves with others like us to see if we measure up.

When comparison rules our lives, we get joy from the wrong places: by beating others at the game instead of experiencing the pure delight of celebrating others' accomplishments. In fact, a benchmark of our hearts is whether we are thankful or resentful when another person succeeds. Oh, most of us are too shrewd to be openly resentful when another person in the company gets the promotion instead of us, or when another parent's child wins acclaim and ours doesn't, but it's precisely in these moments that we have our best opportunity to take an honest inventory of our hearts.

When Cain found himself losing the comparison game, God graciously pointed out his error and offered him another opportunity to do it right. Thankfully, God gives us many opportunities to do it right. When we offer less than our best to God, or when we offer the best with a demanding, reluctant heart, God's Spirit taps us on the shoulder and says, "Hey, why are you angry? Watch out. Sin is crouching at your door. Make a better choice next time. Realize that I've given you everything you enjoy. Acknowledge me as the Lord of your life, and give thanks for what I've done for you. Now, try it again."

In every test, we always come back to the nature of God and our role as his beloved children. When we compare ourselves to others, we assume that we know what's best for us and for them—and we're sure we deserve more than them! But God wants us to focus our hearts totally and only on him. When we get even a glimpse of his greatness and grace, our hearts melt in his love and we gladly give him the best of our flocks. It makes perfect sense.

When my son Dakota was in the first grade, one of his friends had a brother who was in a terrible car accident. The boy needed extensive surgery. The cost was far more than the parents could pay, so the school raised money to help defray the cost. His teacher told the students that if they gave a dollar, they could wear a hat at school that day. That night as I put Dakota to bed, he told me about his friend's brother and the fundraiser the next day. He said, "Dad, would you pray for him?" We prayed, and I kissed him goodnight.

The next morning, I walked into Dakota's room and found him emptying his jar of coins on his bed. He counted the money, and it came to $50. I asked, "Son, what are you going to do with all that money?"

He looked at me like little kids do when they think their fathers don't get it, and he said, "Dad, don't you remember? My friend's brother is having surgery, and they need some money."

I asked, "Son, that's $50. Does that mean you get to wear a hat for 50 days?"

I got the same look again, and he sighed, "Dad, it's not about the hats. My friend's brother needs the money."

Later that morning, Dakota's teacher called to tell me that he had brought $50 to give toward the boy's surgery. She was concerned that I'd be upset, or at least surprised, by his extravagant gift. I explained, "Yes, I know. That's what he wants to do with his money."

She replied, "Wow, that's incredible."

"Yeah," I answered, "he really gets it." When I hung up the phone, I wondered, "But do I get it? Do I understand that God owns it all, and it's not about wearing hats to have fun or impressing people with how much we do for God. It's about giving my very best to Almighty God with no strings attached."

I believe that comparison can be a very strong string attached to everything we do. We can do the right things for the most selfish reasons, but often, we aren't even aware that our motives are rotten until God's Spirit shines his light on the recesses of our hearts. When we give money, time, or talents, what do we expect in return? Do we crave the applause of others and make sure they know what we've done, or is the smile of God reward enough? That morning in Dakota's bedroom, I had a clearer picture of what it means to give ourselves without strings attached. In that way, I hope I can be more like my son.

When we lose the comparison game, few of us get so angry that we kill the one who looks better than us, but many of us commit a gradual spiritual suicide. We harbor resentments against people and against God because someone else has more than we do or gets more praise than we've received. But we fail to realize that these things can't fill the hole in our hearts. Jesus asked, "What good will it be for a man if he gains the whole world, yet forfeits his soul?" (Matthew 16:26) The answer is, of course, nothing. One of the clearest messages in the Bible is that possessions, positions, and popularity can't give us ultimate fulfillment. We find the deepest satisfaction only when we "lose our lives" to "find" them, when we live to serve instead of insisting on our own rights, and when we sense the smile of God. That's all that really matters.

In what areas of life do you find yourself playing the comparison game? Which people do you find yourself comparing to the most? Why?

How does comparison make us proud or resentful (or both)? What is an area of work or service that you desire more applause for the good you are doing?

What does it mean to give and serve "with no strings attached"? What has the Holy Spirit said to you about comparison as you've read today's chapter?

Jesus, you gave with no strings attached. Help me to...

Noah
THE TENACITY TEST

God saw how corrupt the earth had become, for all the people on earth had corrupted their ways. So God said to Noah, "I am going to put an end to all people, for the earth is filled with violence because of them. I am surely going to destroy both them and the earth. So make yourself an ark of cypress wood; make rooms in it and coat it with pitch inside and out" . . . Noah did everything just as God commanded him. (Genesis 6:12-14, 22)

God often uses new Christians in striking ways. When they initiate conversations with friends to tell them about their new life in Christ, many of their friends want to trust Christ, too! When these young Christians pray for God to provide something they need, God often works in powerful ways. These are glorious days to help new believers become grounded in their faith and learn to trust their heavenly Father. Many of us expect these shining moments to keep moving upward in greater and greater intimacy and power for the rest of our lives, but sooner or later, God's curriculum includes other, more difficult tests.

If we walk with God long enough, the day comes when God clearly instructs us to enter a season of preparation. He may want to prepare us for greater effectiveness, and sometimes he instructs us to back away from service for a while as he develops our character and deepens our walk with him. Or he may use this time to prepare those around us so they will be ready to join us when the time is right. Whatever his purpose may be, times of preparation can feel awkward and empty. They are, I believe, some of the most difficult times in our Christian experience, but God uses this classroom to teach us essential lessons. If we fail to perceive these times accurately, we'll resent them, resist them, and quit before we've learned our lessons.

In the early generations after Adam and Eve were escorted out of the Garden, people didn't exactly shine as bright lights of godliness. In one of the most scathing indictments about human nature in the Scriptures, we read this description of the first couple's descendents: "The Lord saw how great man's wickedness on the earth had become, and that every inclination of the thoughts of his heart was only evil all the time" (Genesis 6:5). God decided something had to be done to prevent people from unraveling his plans for humans on earth. We may think watching the evening news shows a lot of evil today, but at that point in history, it was worse—much worse. People were so evil that God decided to wipe out the entire race, except for one family that remained faithful to him.

I'm not sure what line of business Noah had been in, but God stepped in to redirect him. God explained that he was going to "put an end to all people" and "destroy" them. That must have been a shock to Noah, but then God told him to build an enormous boat. He gave him exact dimensions and told him what materials to use. A boat? Building a huge ship on dry ground made absolutely no sense to Noah. There wasn't an ocean or even a lake nearby where it could sail, but Noah trusted God enough to obey him even when he didn't understand the full picture.

For perhaps 100 years, Noah and his sons labored to build the huge ship on dry ground.[4] Day after day, year after year, and decade after

---

4   The Bible doesn't specifically state how long it took Noah to build the ark. Noah is 500 years old when he is first mentioned in Genesis 5:32. When Noah entered the ark, he was 600 years old. The time it took to build the ark would depend on how much time had passed between Genesis 5:32 and the time that God commanded Noah to build the ark (Genesis 6:14-21). At most, it took 100 years.

decade, the men went to work to construct a craft like nothing they had ever seen before. Can you imagine Noah and his sons laboring so long to build the huge ship without a sea in sight? In the conflict between God's clear directive and the seeming absurdity of their task, they faced a stiff test of their tenacity. How long would it take for you or me to quit? I can easily conceive waking up one morning in the 34th year and thinking, "This is ridiculous. Why in the world am I spending so much time working on this thing? Maybe I misunderstood God all those years ago. And besides, I've never even seen a rain that could budge a boat like that!"

Self-doubt may have crept into their thinking, and I can imagine the vicious ridicule they must have endured from their neighbors. Mocking, sarcasm, and outright accusations of insanity—I'm sure they heard every kind of abuse from their homeowners association. Still, they kept building.

When the Ark was complete, they gathered the animals and shut the doors. If I had been Noah at that moment before the rains came, I would have looked around the Ark at my family and all the animals, and I would have thought, "What in the world have I been doing all this time? I'm the laughingstock of the world!" But Noah simply obeyed God and trusted him to do whatever he wanted to do.

In a cataclysmic deluge, God sent rain and flooded the earth, wiping away all the people who had turned their backs on God. Can you imagine what it was like when the waters rose high enough for the boat to float? At that moment, Noah must have thought, "So this is what this ship is about!" His emotions must have run the full gamut, from gratitude that his family was saved from the flood, to vindication that his tenacity was being rewarded, to sorrow for all the people who were drowning outside the boat.

After months on the Ark, the land dried and Noah and his family walked out onto dry ground. For decades, God had prepared these few people to be the remnant of humans who would repopulate the earth. They could have given up so many times, and to be honest, with very good excuses! In spite of all the hard work and ridicule, they tenaciously stayed strong and trusted God.

The Bible uses many words as synonyms for tenacious: faithful, steadfast, firm, or fixed. All of them are used to describe the attitude that says, "No matter what, I'm not going to quit. I may not understand, but God, I trust you anyway." Like Noah, all of us go through times when God is preparing us for greater things. These aren't times when we're so tired and burned out that we've collapsed and need a break. That's a very different issue! No, I'm talking about times when we've been following God, seeing him work through us, but suddenly he takes us out of the battle, perhaps alone in our reflections or perhaps to attend school, but certainly to teach us lessons we couldn't learn when we were in the middle of the battle.

I love the movie *The Karate Kid*. In the story, Daniel is a teenager who wants to date Ali, a cute girl in town. Her ex-boyfriend Johnny is a student of Cobra Kai karate school, where he learns to fight dirty. Daniel tries to learn to fight by reading books about karate at the library, but he's no match for Johnny and his friends. A neighbor, Mr. Miyagi, sees one of the fights when Daniel gets beaten up, and he steps in to protect the boy from the five bullies. Daniel is impressed and thankful, and he asks Mr. Miyagi to teach him.

Mr. Miyagi's training techniques seem odd and out of place to Daniel. He instructs the boy to perform chores such as waxing cars, sanding wood floors, and painting a fence. For each one, he tells Daniel to use specific motions. Daniel, though, doesn't see any connection between his chores and karate. Slowly, his frustration and confusion turn into anger, and he lashes out at Mr. Miyagi. At that moment, the wise old man shows Daniel that each of the chores has taught him important karate moves. The time of preparation proved far more effective than the boy had imagined.

The point of the story about Daniel in *The Karate Kid* is that times of preparation often seem unnecessary and frustrating, but under the direction of God (or a mentor like Mr. Miyagi), we learn valuable skills, and more importantly, rich lessons about life. During those times, we have to be tenacious to stay engaged, open to God's instruction, and responsive to his leading. As Daniel showed us, times of preparation can be very confusing. We may think that we've sinned and we're experiencing the consequences, or worse, we might conclude that God has let us down or abandoned us. Times of preparation, though, are like pruning described in John 15—we've been fruitful, and God wants to equip us for even more effective service. How can we know the difference between the consequences of sin and times of preparation? By talking to a mature believer who knows what each one looks like.

Noah's test was to keep believing God and to keep building the Ark all those years when people ridiculed him, doubts crept in, and no rain came. He had to have a tenacious faith to stay focused and faithful. His time of preparation, though, finally made sense when God unleashed the flood. God used Noah and his family to start over again. All of us are physical and spiritual descendents of the man who passed the test.

We all want to be successful, but success is where preparation and opportunity meet. Without preparation, we simply won't be successful.

As you look back now, what have been some times in your life when you were being prepared for a bigger purpose?

During times of preparation, what are some things that might make us feel like quitting?

What do we know about God's character and his purposes that may help us remain tenacious during our times of preparation?

What have been some areas in your life when confusion and frustration have caused you to lose your tenacity? If you're at that point now, what steps can you take to gain it back, specifically in those areas?

Father, I need to be tenacious to follow you when...

Abraham
THE PURE HEART TEST

Some time later God tested Abraham. He said to him, "Abraham!" "Here I am," he replied. Then God said, "Take your son, your only son, Isaac, whom you love, and go to the region of Moriah. Sacrifice him there as a burnt offering on one of the mountains I will tell you about." (Genesis 22:1-2)

Has there ever been a more excruciating, gut-wrenching test than the one God gave Abraham? Let's retrace the story of Abraham and Isaac to see how they got to this moment.

God called Abraham from Ur in the desert of present day Iraq, and he promised to make a great nation out of his descendents. Abraham and his wife Sarah were old (he was 75 and she was about 65) and childless, but they accepted God's call and headed toward the Promised Land. I'm sure this couple knew a thing or two about when it was optimum for people to have children. They were already old, and the clock was ticking. They probably expected Sarah to get pregnant right away, but that's not how it worked out. Year after year passed without a child. Sarah finally got fed up with the unanswered prayers, so she came up with a plan to help God out. Since she hadn't gotten pregnant, she decided to send her maid into the bedroom with Abraham. Hagar soon became pregnant and had a child, Ishmael.

God, however, didn't agree with Sarah's revised plan for their lives. He sent three angels to them, and they promised Abraham that his wife would have a child in a year. Sarah was eavesdropping on the conversation, and when she heard their promise, she laughed. The angel's promise, though, wasn't a joke. Even as a 90 year-old woman, Sarah became pregnant and had a son, Isaac, a name that means "laughter."

This, as you can imagine, was no ordinary family. The parents had received a promise from God, but they had waited 25 years for the promise to be fulfilled. Now, in their old age, they had the son they had dreamed about for all those years. As Isaac grew, his father's love for him gradually consumed his heart. The boy, God's promised gift, crowded God out of the center of Abraham's affections and became an idol.

We read in the Bible that God is described as a "jealous God." That, some of us assume, just can't be. Jealousy seems to be petty, selfish, and wrong. How can God be jealous? But there are two types of jealousy. One is the selfish kind that hates it when someone else gets the affection we want; the other is noble and right, like a husband protecting his marriage against a rival who wants to steal his wife's affections. If the husband didn't protect their relationship, we'd wonder if he loved her at all. That's the kind of jealousy God has for us. He wants our hearts to be completely his, and when our affections wander, he does whatever it takes to bring us back.

Abraham's affections had drifted away from God and were now absorbed in his son. God's means of testing can be subtle, but sometimes, he quickly gets to the heart of the matter to cut out the cancer in a single stroke. Instead of letting the disease linger, he deals with it dramatically and quickly. God spoke to Abraham and gave him a clear command: Take your son to the mountain and kill him.

Can you imagine the impact this word from God had on the old father? It must have hit him like a sledgehammer, but he didn't complain and he didn't run. He saddled the donkey, cut wood for an offering, and took Isaac and two servants on a trip to the mountain. Mt. Moriah was a three-day journey. During the journey, I can imagine what was going on in Abraham's mind. It must have been agonizing. "Surely," he must have thought, "I misunderstood God." No, his instructions were clear. "Maybe I can turn back and talk about it with God." No, there's no need in that. The writer to the Hebrews tells us that Abraham believed that God could raise Isaac from the dead, so he was willing to go through with the deed (see Hebrews 11:19).

When they got to the mountain, Abraham built an altar, placed his son on it, and raised his knife to slay him. Suddenly, the angel of the Lord called out to stop him: " 'Do not lay a hand on the boy,' he said. 'Do not do anything to him. Now I know that you fear God, because you have not withheld from me your son, your only son' " (Genesis 22:12).

God had taken Abraham to the brink to see if he would actually be obedient and kill his beloved son. (I wonder what was going through Isaac's mind all this time.) God provided a ram for the sacrifice, and Abraham and Isaac walked down the mountain and traveled back home. Both of them, I'm sure, had been transformed by God's test.

God designed this moment in Abraham's life to purify his motives and bring his wandering heart back to him. The hearts of many people are filled with idols of money, power, sex, and all kinds of other things, but the message of this story is different: God's promised gift, the son that Abraham had waited for so long, had become more important to him than God. When the gift replaces the Giver, God steps in to reorient our priorities.

What is the most precious gift God has given you? Perhaps it's a child, or maybe it's a spouse or a career you enjoy. In many cases, it's a dream come true, someone or something we've longed for. We may have prayed and waited for years. Finally, God gave us our heart's desire, and we're supremely grateful. If these people, possessions, or roles gradually shove God off the throne of our lives, however, they become idols instead of gifts. Because we're human and it's very easy to give our hearts fully to a spouse, a child, a job, or a possession we can see instead of an invisible God, virtually all of us face this test sooner or later.

Elisabeth Elliot often has piercing insights about spiritual life. We are wise, she observes, to loosen our grip on God's gifts so our hands can grasp something far more valuable. In *Keep a Quiet Heart*, she wrote,

> "Money [and any other possession or person who may take God's place in our hearts] holds terrible power when it is loved. It can blind us, shackle us, fill us with anxiety and fear, torment our days and nights with misery, wear us out with chasing it. . . . Poverty has not been my experience, but God has allowed in the lives of each of us some sort of loss, the withdrawal of something we valued, in order that we may learn to offer ourselves a little more willingly, to allow the touch of death on one more thing we have clutched so tightly, and thus know fullness and freedom and joy that much sooner."[5]

As we see in Abraham's life, the thing we want most from God has the potential of becoming too precious to us. The gift certainly isn't evil, but God wants our hearts to be loyal to him. As a loving Father or husband of the bride of Christ, he takes away (or at least threatens to take away) anything that replaces him in our affections.

My friend Chris Railey and his wife Cara longed to have children. They prayed, they wept, and they cried out to God to give them a child. He told me, "We felt God's plan for our lives involved having children. We planned, saved money, and prayed, but the pain and desperation was not in getting pregnant that first time—it was everything that happened after Cara got pregnant. When we found out we were going to have a baby, we immediately got down on our knees to commit this child to God, but we had no concept of what that really meant. It's easy to say

---

5   Elisabeth Elliott, *Keep a Quiet Heart*, (Revell, 2004), pp. 38-39.

but hard to do. God put that prayer to the test." Chris and Cara were thrilled, and they were very grateful. He told me, "From the moment we found out Cara was pregnant, we said, 'Lord, thank you so much. We give this child to you.' "

Two months later, though, the doctors told Cara that the baby had died in her womb. They were crushed, but they held on to God and each other. Before too long, she became pregnant again, but several weeks later, she lost this child, too. Two more times, this dear couple's hopes were dashed by a doctor's dismal news. During all this time, Chris and Cara felt confused and hurt because their dream had been shattered over and over again. Chris told me about a particularly painful moment: "On the day we found out she was having the fourth miscarriage, I stood in the kitchen with Cara, and I told God I may have misunderstood him. I thought he wanted us to have children, but maybe I was wrong. At that moment, we determined to trust God even if he didn't provide children for us. We surrendered our dream for our family and put ourselves in his hands, with no demands and no expectations."

For Chris and Cara, surrendering their dream of having children was a turning point in their lives and their marriage. The crushing disappointments could have caused them to become hardened, but they chose to be tender toward God. The fires of heartache threatened to consume them, but instead, they chose to trust God, and he used it to purify their hearts like nothing else they had ever experienced. Though they no longer expected God to give them a child, the Lord had other plans. Chris and Cara now have three wonderful children who are gifts from God, and whose place in their parents' lives will always be secondary to the God who took pains to purify their hearts.

As you've read this chapter, have you had any thoughts like, "Man, I sure hope God doesn't touch him (or her or this or that)!" If you've had that thought, that person or thing may be too important to you. Take time to reflect on the rightful place of the Giver and the gift, and ask God to give you courage to put him first. If you don't, you can expect a loving God to test you and reorient your priorities.

Who are some people and things that are gifts from God but can become too important in believers' lives? How about in your own life?

What are some signs that we're clinging too much to those people, things, or roles more than we cling to God?

Is there any gift that threatens to replace the Giver in your life? What steps do you need to take to put things back in right order, placing God as the higher priority than any gift?

Father, you are a noble and jealous God who wants to be in the center of my affections. Today I ask you to...

Isaac
THE FAMILY LEGACY
TEST

Now there was a famine in the land—besides the earlier famine of Abraham's time—and Isaac went to Abimelech king of the Philistines in Gerar. The Lord appeared to Isaac and said, "Do not go down to Egypt; live in the land where I tell you to live. Stay in this land for a while, and I will be with you and will bless you. For to you and your descendants I will give all these lands and will confirm the oath I swore to your father Abraham." (Genesis 26:1-3)

I believe modeling is the most powerful teaching tool in the world. We can tell people what to do, and we can preach to them until we're blue in the face and their eyes roll back in their heads, but having people watch us in real-life situations is far more powerful. As parents, our children are far more likely to do as we do instead of doing as we say. Their attention drifts in and out as we talk to them, but they watch our actions with eagle eyes.

In every family, habits and values are passed down from one generation to the next. After a fairly normal time of experimentation and opposition in the teenage years, young adults often copy their parents' hobbies, politics, food choices, parenting style, type of friends, ways of communicating, and every other important aspect of life. How many times have you heard people say to someone, "You sound just like your

Mom," or "You act just like your Dad." I'm not sure if generational rep-
lication is more nature than nurture, but I suspect both have a lot to do
with it.

For some of us, our parents' modeling was incredibly noble and
strong. We watched them carefully and learned the value of trusting
God, loving people, serving others, speaking truth, and valuing humility
and justice. Others are on the other end of the spectrum. We suffered
some form of abuse or abandonment, and our lives today are colored by
those painful experiences. Most of us, however, didn't experience the
extremes of either end of the parenting spectrum. Our parents modeled
some good traits, but they failed at some important ones, too. Our task
is to figure out which ones we want to keep and which ones we want to
change. Our own lives, and the future of our children, depend on it.

In the Genesis account, we find Isaac facing a choice between his
father's modeling and God's direction. He's the child of the promise,
the son of Abraham and Sarah, who grew up watching his parents and
hearing stories about their journey of faith. Years after the supreme test
of Abraham's faith on Mt. Moriah, Sarah died and Isaac married Rebekah. Later, a famine gripped the land. God appeared to Isaac and
repeated the promise he had given his father to bless the world through
his descendents, but he told Isaac not to go to Egypt to find food. Years
before, God had told Abraham to go to the Promised Land, but when he
faced a famine, he fled to Egypt. Now, what would Isaac do? Would he
follow the path of his father, or would he obey God? Isaac decided to do
what God commanded, and he stayed in Gerar.

Chalk one up for Isaac. He passed the first test, but another one
soon followed. In Gerar, some tough guys asked him about the beautiful
woman who was with him. It was his wife Rebekah. Isaac responded,
" 'She is my sister,' because he was afraid to say, 'She is my wife.' He
thought, 'The men of this place might kill me on account of Rebekah,
because she is beautiful.' "

Twice in Abraham's life he faced the same threat—once in Egypt when the pharaoh's officers saw Sarah's beauty, and another time years later when Abimelech saw her and wanted to marry her. Both times, Abraham caved in to the perceived threats and told them Sarah was his sister, and both times, God had to intervene to keep men from violating her. Now, when Isaac faced the same problem, he took the same cowardly course of action, lying about Rebekah the same way his father had lied about Sarah years before. This time, Isaac failed the test.

Our tests related to family legacy come in two forms: Will we follow the honorable patterns our parents have set in front of us, and will we have the courage to change the ones that are harmful and destructive? Our spouse and children, and generations to come, depend on us to make good choices. Let me offer a few suggestions.

First, sit up and notice the patterns in your family. How did your parents resolve conflict? How did they treat you and your siblings? Did they build an environment that valued truth and grace, or did they lash out in anger or withdraw in fear? What type of work ethic did they have? How did they steward their finances? What were they passionate about? For better or worse, we've internalized a whole set of values and behaviors as they served as examples to follow. Our first task, then, is to be observant about the strengths and weaknesses of the way our parents modeled life for us.

Second, treasure the noble, good, and courageous traits they passed down to you. Think of the wonderful stories they told about themselves and their ancestors, and thank God for the good memories and traditions they gave you when you were growing up. Don't take these for granted.

And third, create a plan to heal any damage and remove harmful patterns of behavior, attitudes, and relationships. It's easy, very easy, to keep reacting in the same way time after time, year after year. Those deeply ingrained patterns won't change with a wish. Genuine transformation requires clarity of thought, a plan of action, and courage to take steps to carve out a new legacy for your spouse and kids. Because modeling is so powerful, breaking a destructive family cycle is one of the most difficult things anyone can do, but I know hundreds, maybe thousands, of courageous men and women who have done it. Healing a deep wound, though, always leaves a scar. God has delivered us and forgiven us, and he does wonderful things in our lives to bring light out of darkness, but until we see him face to face, we still carry the scars from our wounds. Don't despise these scars. They are marks of healing and hope, and they remind us of how far God has brought us.

When I think of painful or destructive family legacies, the image I have in mind is of a grocery cart with one wheel out of alignment. Whenever you push it, the cart angles to one side. People may use it, but they'll fight with it up and down every aisle until they get to the cashier. Until it's fixed, nothing will change. It will keep pulling to one side day after day until someone notices the problem, grabs his tools, and changes the alignment.

In the incredible grace of God, he's willing to use every difficulty we've experienced to deepen our walks with him and give us a platform to speak into others lives. In the opening verses of his second letter to the Corinthians, Paul observed that God "comforts us in all our troubles, so that we can comfort those in any trouble with the comfort we ourselves have received from God" (2 Corinthians 1:4). A seminary professor commented on this phenomenon and said that the most difficult problems we face in the first half of our lives will be—if we let God heal our wounds and give us wisdom—the source of our greatest ministry the last half of our lives. People who have been deeply wounded and experienced God's healing have more compassion for hurting people than anybody I know. God never wastes our pain. He uses it to draw us deeper into a relationship with him and to touch people's lives. I shared these thoughts with my friend Leonard Sweet, and he sent me an email that said, "Your tests become your testimony." In a flash of inspiration, I wrote him back and told him, "Yes, and your mess becomes your message!"

The principle of modeling and family legacy applies to every aspect of life. On a lighter note, my Dad is a wonderful role model in many areas, but he didn't exactly pass down the genes to be a great athlete. When I was a boy, I tried to play sports, but I wasn't very good—and that might be too positive about my abilities! Once when I was playing on a basketball team, Dad sat in the stands yelling, "Go, son, go!"

I turned around and said, "Dad, I'm sitting on the bench. I'm not even in the game."

I only got to play if we were up by 20 or down by 20 with a minute remaining in the game. My son Dillon, though, is a terrific athlete. He's become a starter on his varsity football team at a 5A school. When my friends come to his games and sit near us, they are well aware of my lack of athletic ability, so at every touchdown, field goal, and kickoff, they yell, "Dillon, break the curse! Break the curse!" It's true. Hilarious, but true.

My Dad was a terrific father and a gifted leader, and it has been his aim throughout our lives to pass on everything he knows to his kids. On many occasions, he told us, "I want to give you everything I've got, and I hope you can do far better than I've done. Don't settle for my level of success. Trust God and do more than either of us could possibly imagine."

That's a fantastic legacy for any son or daughter.

What are the positive traits your parents modeled for you? How well are you replicating these for your family? What are some positive behaviors that you have observed in other families that you'd like to incorporate into your family?

What are some painful, harmful attitudes and behaviors your parents modeled? How have these affected you?

Consider the three elements of legacy (notice the patterns, treasure the noble traits, and have courage to change the harmful ones) and write a plan to change one thing.

Jesus, thank you that my parents modeled these things for me...

Jacob
THE HONESTY TEST

When the messengers returned to Jacob, they said, "We went to your brother Esau, and now he is coming to meet you, and four hundred men are with him."

In great fear and distress Jacob divided the people who were with him into two groups, and the flocks and herds and camels as well. He thought, "If Esau comes and attacks one group, the group that is left may escape." (Genesis 32:6-8)

All of Jacob's long and twisted life came down to the day when he had nowhere to hide, nowhere to run, and nobody to turn to—except God. He had tried to manipulate and con his way through life, and he was incredibly successful, but there comes a day when people have to face the consequences of a life of deception. This day was the nightmare Jacob had dreaded.

It certainly wasn't an isolated incident. He hadn't "slipped up" just a time or two. No, his life was a fabric of lies. In fact, his name meant "deceiver" or "schemer." Today, we might hear of someone like him and call him "slick." It's not a complimentary term! No matter what it took, Jacob made sure he got his way. He had gotten his older brother Esau to sign away his birthright for a bowl of stew when he was famished. And when Isaac, his father, approached his death and was ready to bestow the blessing of the firstborn on Esau, Jacob and his mother orchestrated an elaborate ruse to fool his dad. To look and feel like his hairy brother, Jacob put animal skins on his arms and shoulders, and his mother cooked game the way Esau would prepare a special dish for his father. The scheme worked, and Isaac gave his younger son his brother's coveted blessing. Not surprisingly, this theft enraged his brother, and Jacob had to flee for his life.

You might think that Jacob would see the error of his ways, but he wasn't through with his deceit. He ran to Laban, his uncle, and lived with him tending sheep. Laban had two daughters. The older one, Leah, was, to put it kindly, a plain-looking girl. Jacob had eyes for Rachel, Laban's gorgeous younger daughter. This time, however, the deceiver met his match. Jacob said he'd work for seven years for Rachel's hand, but on the wedding night, he got drunk. The next morning when he opened his eyes, he looked over next to him and "Behold, it was Leah."

When Jacob confronted Laban about the fraud, Laban shrugged and said, "Hey, it's not our custom to marry off the younger daughter first. If you want Rachel, you can have her, but you'll have to work another seven years." (Imagine how Leah felt when she overheard this conversation!)

Jacob was willing to do anything to have Rachel, so he agreed to the deal, but with the stipulation that he could keep speckled and spotted sheep and goats. Still up to his old ways, he manipulated the breeding of the flocks so that many of the sheep and goats now belonged to him. When Laban's sons realized Jacob was taking everything they owned, he became afraid and fled with his two wives, their maids, and their many sons.

Jacob now had nowhere to go. His only hope was to return home, but he faced his brother's wrath. He sent word ahead to Esau that he was coming — he didn't want to surprise him. When the messenger returned, he reported that Esau was coming with 400 men! Suddenly, all of the schemes that had seemed so successful now were debts coming due.

Jacob prepared elaborate and expensive gifts to appease his brother, but he didn't have confidence that they'd work. As a last resort, he decided to turn to God. That night, he crossed the river and wrestled with God. Of course, God could have easily overwhelmed human strength, but a display of divine power wasn't his purpose. God wanted to demonstrate to Jacob that devising plots to con people out of what was rightly theirs isn't the best way to live. Integrity and honesty provide the only solid platform for relationships—with the Lord and with people. To remind him to keep depending on God's wisdom and strength, the Lord touched Jacob's hip and put it out of joint. For the rest of his life, he walked with a limp, but he never forgot the lesson he learned that night. From then on, he faced many challenges, but he never resorted to deceit. He must have learned his lesson because God changed his name to Israel, which may mean "strives with God" or "prince of God."

We shouldn't look at Jacob and shake our heads in disgust. We face the same challenges he did, but with different names, faces, and situations. Dishonesty is taking the easy way out. Too often, we use deceit to get what we want without paying the price of responsibility. We may not deceive our fathers to steal a sibling's birthright, but we face countless smaller choices every day.

- Do we gossip to secretly put someone down hoping to make ourselves look better?

- Do we neglect to tell the whole truth when our spouse, friend, or employer asks a question?

- Do we add a personal expense when we're filling out a company expense report?

- Do we fail to include some income or add sham deductions on our taxes?

- Do we stretch the truth to appear a little better and make others appear a little worse?

- Do we hide some behavior hoping no one will ever find out?

- Do we face a critical moment of truth and choose to lie to avoid responsibility?

Every deceit ultimately causes negative consequences. Like Jacob, we may become pretty skilled at lying, shading the truth, and telling half-truths, and it may be a long time before we're caught red handed. But sooner or later, the day will come in our lives when "Esau is coming with 400 men." On that day, we can panic, run like crazy, point fingers, or finally turn to God.

Changing a lifetime of deceit doesn't happen easily. Some of us have been secretly and discretely shading the truth all our lives. Until now, we've gotten away with it, but it's time to change. Those habits become deeply ingrained in us, and we often have to wrestle with God for a long time so that we become convinced that we simply have to change. If these habits have controlled our lives, God may have to put a hip out of joint as a continual reminder that we need to trust him and speak the truth all day every day. Even after a lifetime of deceit, God didn't give up on Jacob. He still planned to use Jacob, now called Israel, as a link in the chain of the nation's history and the lineage of the Messiah.

I believe God brings us to a point when we've tried everything imaginable to make life work, but we've failed. Now, we're desperate and open to him like never before. Years ago, my father-in-law, Glen Anderson, was an alcoholic and drug addict. His life was a complete mess. Our family was staying at his home one Christmas many years ago. I got up in the night and went into the kitchen, and he was standing there. Since I'd known him, we never had a deep, personal conversation. We talked only about sports and the weather. But that night, he was ready to talk about God and his life. Like Jacob, Glen was wrestling with God at night. He said, "Scott, I'm not sure what to do about God. If I trust him and he doesn't come through for me, I don't know where I'd go from there." He had used alcohol and drugs to numb his pain and make him forget the damage he had caused. For weeks, he had considered turning his life over to God, but he realized that this was his last shot at making sense of life. If God didn't come through, he'd have nothing left at all. "Scott, please don't give up on me," he asked.

"Don't worry, Glen," I reassured him. "I won't ever give up on you, and neither will God."

Glen must have said those words because he knew his wrestling wasn't over. For the next three years, he still guarded his addictions and shut God out of his life. Addictions always involve a lot of deceit. Addicts spend their days trying to fool family members and employers, and they tell themselves lies like, "I can quit anytime I want to," and "I'm not really hurting anybody."

There may be many reasons people enter recovery, but there's a single motivation that's common to all of them: desperation. After these years, Glen's level of desperation finally exceeded his level of fear. He turned to God and experienced God's love, forgiveness, and strength. Over the next couple of years, Glen and three of Jenni's siblings came to live with us. They dealt with their addictions, came to Christ, and started living for God. Glen is now the head of our church's recovery ministry. Does he see through people's excuses and lies? You bet he does, but he doesn't condemn them. He loves those people because he knows what they're going through—their fears and their hopes.

Glen's life had been full of deceit, but God met him, wrestled with him, and changed his life. God had a plan to change the scheming Jacob into a godly leader, and God transformed Glen in the same way. The good news of grace is that nobody is beyond God's attention and affection.

Some of us are major league deceivers like Jacob and Glen, but all of us face the test of honesty every day. God delights when we turn to him and courageously speak the truth.

What are some ways people try to deceive others? What do they hope to gain from their deceit?

In what way was it a mark of God's grace that he put Jacob's hip out of joint?

What are some ways you lie, exaggerate, or tell half-truths? Why do you think it's tempting for you to avoid telling the whole truth in these areas? What steps can you take to change these patterns?

Have you been completely honest in answering these questions? Why or why not?

Jesus, you are the truth, and I want my life to be...

Joseph
THE READINESS TEST

He restored the chief cupbearer to his position, so that he once again put the cup into the pharaoh's hand, but he hanged the chief baker, just as Joseph had said to them in his interpretation. The chief cupbearer, however, did not remember Joseph; he forgot him. (Genesis 40:21-23)

When I think about Joseph, my mind drifts to those countless moments the Scriptures don't talk about—times when any of us (including me) would have been tempted to feel completely abandoned, hopeless, and helpless. Times of isolation and disappointment are some of the most difficult tests we face. For a while, we hang in there and trust something good will come along, but as hope gradually fades, anticipation can turn to resentment. To me, the most striking feature of Joseph's life isn't that he became prime minister of Egypt, but that he was spiritually and emotionally ready for that role even though he experienced disappointment again and again.

Joseph was Jacob's 11th son, and he was the apple of his father's eye. When he was a boy, he had two dreams about his parents and brothers someday bowing down to him. Foolishly, he told them about the dream. Get the picture: If you're the favorite child in a family, you don't want to give your siblings any ammo to resent you even more! His brothers despised him, and one day when he went out to check on their work, they decided to do away with him. Some planned to kill him then and there, but soon they devised a different plan. The brothers sold Joseph as a slave to a Midianite caravan headed to Egypt. They disguised their treachery by dipping his coat in sheep's blood and told their dad that a wild animal had killed him.

Potiphar, a local Egyptian official, bought Joseph. He recognized the boy's organizational skills, and he put him in charge of his household. The problem was that Potiphar wasn't in charge of his own marriage. His wife tried to seduce the handsome young Hebrew. When Joseph fled the house, he left his clothes in her clutching hands. The boy quickly found himself in an Egyptian prison. At this point, it would have been easy to give up, but he kept trusting God. The young man showed such administrative talents that the warden put him in charge of the prison.

Some time later, the pharaoh had trouble with his domestics, so he threw his baker and cupbearer into prison. There, the two men had vivid and alarming dreams. They had no idea what to make of them, but Joseph did. He interpreted the dreams. The cupbearer, he foretold from the dream, would be restored to his honored position, but the baker would meet a very different fate: execution. Joseph pleaded with the cupbearer to remember him when he got out. Later, the events happened just as Joseph predicted, but the cupbearer forgot about him.

Forgot! Can you believe that? How in the world could the cupbearer forget Joseph after he had interpreted his dream and predicted everything that eventually happened? I can't imagine forgetting someone like that—it must have been the wine. This is the moment that is most poignant to me. It's tragic that his brothers betrayed him, wanted to kill him, and then sold him into slavery and lied to their father. As a slave, Joseph was honorable and efficient, and he resisted having sex with his owner's wife. What was his reward for remaining trustworthy?

A dungeon. For years, he languished in prison, serving the warden effectively but longing to get out. He had one good chance to escape the dungeon, but the only man who could help him forgot about him. At that point, those dreams of his childhood must have seemed like distant memories, but we never read that Joseph gave up on God or God's plan for him. Never. That's the most amazing thing about Joseph.

When the pharaoh had disturbing dreams and his wise men couldn't interpret them, the cupbearer finally remembered and reported how Joseph had accurately interpreted the dream of the baker and his own. When Joseph correctly revealed and interpreted the pharaoh's dreams, he put him in charge of the entire kingdom! During seven years of plenty, Joseph gave orders to store grain for the upcoming famine. Then, a year or two into it, a striking event took place: His brothers came to Egypt looking for food.

Joseph had been incredibly resilient all those years, trusting God when most of us would have given up in despair. But now, the ones who had betrayed him came to the palace. He had every reason to get revenge, but he didn't. In one of the most amazing acts of self-control in all of history, he tested his brothers to see if the years had changed them. Through a series of events, he found they were unwilling to give up their youngest brother, Benjamin, to save their own skins. They had finally learned their lesson, so Joseph revealed himself to them. When their father died, the brothers wondered if Joseph would use this heartbreaking moment as an excuse to punish them. "But Joseph said to them, 'Don't be afraid. Am I in the place of God? You intended to harm me, but God intended it for good to accomplish what is now being done, the saving of many lives. So then, don't be afraid. I will provide for you and your children.' And he reassured them and spoke kindly to them" (Genesis 50:19-21). Joseph had been unwilling to give up in despair during a prolonged season of emptiness. Instead, he stayed strong in his faith. Because he was ready, the nation of Egypt was saved, his family was rescued from famine, and the fledgling nation of Israel endured.

Joseph was ready when the pharaoh called him because he was convinced in the depths of his soul that God had a good plan for him. Betrayal, slavery, prison, and abandonment couldn't dissolve his faith that God still ruled in heaven and on earth, and someday, he would make things right. With that confidence, nothing could shake Joseph's faith. Through it all, he was ready to respond promptly and wisely when the time came.

Centuries later, the apostle Paul described how it was possible for him to always be ready to respond in faith to any situation. He could only do that, he explained, by seeing life with spiritual eyes, seeing beyond the hurt, disappointment, and turmoil around him, and trusting that God would have his way. He wrote the Corinthians: "Therefore we do not lose heart. Though outwardly we are wasting away, yet inwardly we are being renewed day by day. For our light and momentary troubles are achieving for us an eternal glory that far outweighs them all. So we fix our eyes not on what is seen, but on what is unseen. For what is seen is temporary, but what is unseen is eternal" (2 Corinthians 4:16-18).

One of the lessons we learn from the life of Joseph is that God never promised to protect us from harm. We live in the real world, and we suffer because of our humanity, the sins of others, a fallen creation, and the forces of evil. Joseph, Paul, Jesus, and believers throughout the ages have had to face times of testing—sometimes in terrifying moments of attack, but often in the long, slow pressure cooker of loneliness. These test whether our faith is real or not. How do you and I meet the readiness tests in our lives? In other words: What does it take to make us give up and quit in despair? Some of us face long seasons of emptiness and heartache because of sickness, a loveless marriage, a prodigal child, a shattered career, or some other chronic problem. I'm not suggesting that we should never have emotions of sadness or doubt, but those feelings provide points of choice. Will we give in to self-pity and anger, or will our painful emotions be a springboard for us to focus the eyes of our hearts on truths we can't see, spiritual and eternal truths? Paul says that our heartaches today are "light and momentary troubles," and if we trust God through them, they result in "an eternal glory that far outweighs them all." Paul's glowing theology is shown in the narrative of Joseph's experience. He didn't just know it in his head; he lived it out every day as a son, as a slave, as a prisoner, and as prime minister. No matter what happened, he was ready because he kept his eyes on God instead of his painful circumstances.

My friend and mentor Dr. Samuel Chand traveled to India, and when I saw him after his trip, he gave me an intricately carved ivory female elephant, crafted so you could see a baby elephant inside it. He said, "Scott, when I saw this, it reminded me of you." I thought, "Man, I'm not that fat!" But he explained, "Elephants are the largest land animals in the world, and the gestation period of a baby elephant is 22 months, the longest of any land animal. Pastor Scott, you have such a big dream and vision that it's going to take longer for you to see it come about. Don't give up!"

God's vision for Joseph required a long time and lots of patience. He may have been tempted many times to give up, but he didn't. He passed the readiness test.

What are some of the reasons that people give up on a dream or a vision that they were once so excited to see happen?

What can you imagine Joseph told himself day after day as a slave and in prison to reinforce his faith to keep himself ready?

What dream or vision did you once have that you haven't followed through on or have given up on? Do you think God wants you to hold on to that dream? If you do, what do you need to do to pick that dream back up?

What do you need to do to prepare your mind and heart to endure tough tests so you'll be ready to respond to God?

Father, it's easy to give up when times are hard for a long time. Help me to...

Moses
THE SURRENDER TEST

> One day, after Moses had grown up, he went out to where his own people were and watched them at their hard labor. He saw an Egyptian beating a Hebrew, one of his own people. Glancing this way and that and seeing no one, he killed the Egyptian and hid him in the sand. (Exodus 2:11-12)

As a man who learned his lessons the hard way, Peter wrote, "God opposes the proud but gives grace to the humble." Moses and Peter had their moments of spiritual glory, but they got there by going through a grueling process of purification. Moses was a prince of Egypt. He lived in splendor, enjoying the acclaim of his adoptive family and the kingdom. He knew, however, that he was a Hebrew, and when he became an adult, he wanted to right the wrongs being done to his people. He watched an Egyptian taskmaster beating a defenseless Hebrew slave, and his anger boiled. He made sure no one was watching, and he murdered the Egyptian.

But someone *was* watching. When the news spread to the pharaoh, Moses had to get out of town to let things cool off. God's plan, though, wasn't just to bring some distance between Moses and the Egyptian authorities; God intended to use 40 long years in the desert to change Moses' life. The first test of his life was over the problem of his people in slavery, but Moses had arrogantly taken things in his own hands, with disastrous results.

Lessons on pride and humility aren't easy ones. They often require radical spiritual surgery and long periods of rehabilitation. That was God's curriculum for Moses. For decades, he tended smelly sheep and lived in a tent instead of enjoying the riches of Egypt. During those years, God gradually tenderized Moses' heart. After 40 long, lonely years, God was ready to test Moses again.

It's hard to imagine the scene of a bush on fire but not being consumed. Moses probably rubbed his eyes and thought the desert heat was getting to him, but when God spoke out of the bush, he knew this wasn't a mirage! God called Moses to do the very thing he had tried to do on his own years before: free the slaves in Egypt. But by now, Moses had learned his lesson too well. Instead of running off cocksure of himself, he was filled with self-doubt. He may have thought back to that event so many years before when he tried to help one slave and was forced to flee. And now God wants him to free *all* the slaves? No, that just doesn't make sense. I can almost hear him whisper to himself, "No, I'm not the guy." He asked God, "Who am I to lead your people out of Egypt?" He was sure hoping God's answer would be: "Not you!"

God assured him, "I will be with you."

Then Moses found another excuse. He asked, "What if they don't listen?"

God responded, "Tell them I Am has sent you."

Even the pronouncement of God's name and character weren't enough to invigorate the timid Moses. He then asked, "What if they don't believe me?"

It seems that God had had enough conversation. He showed Moses a number of miracles to prove his power, but even that didn't convince the reluctant prophet. Moses thought about his years of silence tending sheep, and he reported, "But God, I'm not a skilled speaker."

God reminded him that he had created mouths and given people the ability to speak. Even at that point, Moses was still looking for a way out. He suggested that God send someone else. God must have shrugged his shoulders and sighed at Moses' timidity, but he offered to send Aaron, his brother, with him.

Moses failed his first test because of his arrogance, and he almost failed his second test because of his fear and doubt. Finally, he mustered the courage to surrender his life to God, and he headed toward Egypt. There, he faced many more tests. His first attempts to free the slaves resulted in even harsher treatment from the Egyptians, so the slaves became angry with Moses. Time after time, the pharaoh hardened his heart against the deliverer, until finally God sent the Angel of Death to slay the firstborn sons of the land on the night of Passover. The pharaoh let the slaves go, but he pursued them to the sea and threatened to kill them all. Again, Moses faced a test. Would he react in anger and lead a charge against the soldiers? Would he shrink in fear and passively accept defeat? Or would he trust God to do what only God could do. This time, Moses responded in faith, and the nation was saved by another miracle.

Their time in the desert wasn't exactly a day of golf at Palm Springs. Moses had to deal with perhaps two million people grumbling about the food, complaining about the water, and rebelling against his leadership. Each of these moments were tests of his resolve to surrender to God's will or revert back to his arrogant wrath or timidity. Most of the time, he held tight to God, but sometimes, his anger got the best of him. Through the ages, though, only King David rivals Moses as a leader of the Jewish nation. He certainly wasn't perfect, but he faced his heart's twin evils, pride and doubt, and chose to surrender his life to God again and again.

Human nature pushes us to one extreme or the other: angrily demanding our own way or giving up on life and becoming passive. God calls us to a third way, surrendering our lives to God's leadership and having the courage to trust him wherever he leads. Each of us faces this test, sometimes in monumental turning points, but more often in the choices we make each day. We can say, "Lord, I'm yours. I trust you to lead me, and I want you to be in the spotlight, not me." But our pride wants to say, "Hey, I want to be in the spotlight, and I'll figure things out on my own. And besides, God, you need me!" Peter says that "God opposes" people with this attitude—and that sounds pretty serious to me! Timidity is the opposite, but just as serious, reaction: "I'm no good, and I can't do anything right. There's no use even trying." That attitude also hurts God's heart because it's rooted in unbelief. Surrendering our lives to God every day results in great freedom, and it enables us to tap into God's awesome power, but it requires the rare combination of courage and humility. If we surrender, God promises to be with us, to equip us, and to see us through every trial.

John Houston is a friend of mine who went to Bible College to get a pastoral degree and ended up working in the national office of his denomination, but God gave him a dream about doing something completely different. He wanted to be a homebuilder, a role full of risks and far from the safety of his previous job. With the heart of a lion, John launched out. His vision wasn't just to make money by building houses, but to touch lives with the message of Christ. He and a group of people prayed together over every lot in every subdivision, and God gave them remarkable answers. Neighbors came to faith, broken families were reconciled, and God stimulated the faith of countless people. Like Moses, John discovered that surrendering to God led to greater risks, but also to greater fulfillment than he ever imagined.

Four women in our church—Rhonda Abshere, Keela Narramore, Anna Bazan-Parker, and Sonia Gooding—went on an international missions trip, and God used it to change the direction of their lives. They had never spoken in public before, but when the leader asked them to speak, they surrendered their fears, stood up, and told how Christ had touched their hearts. God used them in powerful ways, and they began inviting others to join them on other trips. Their enthusiasm and vision continued to grow, and these four women devoted their lives to missions. In fact, two of them left their business interests so they could spend more time leading mission trips. Today, they take women to far off lands to touch people with Christ's message of forgiveness and hope. The point isn't that they left their secular jobs and went into ministry. It's that they surrendered their hearts to God and did what he directed them to do. When God spoke to them, they went into full-time ministry, but when God spoke to John Houston, he left the ministry to enter the business world. All of them were answering God's call to follow him with all their hearts.

The test of surrender isn't about titles or roles, and it isn't even about effectiveness. It's about listening to God's voice and answering with an affirmative, "Yes, Lord. I'm ready to follow you wherever you lead."

What are some symptoms of pride in people's lives? What are some signs of timidity? In what ways are both a lack of surrender to God?

How do pride and timidity keep individuals from fulfilling God's purposes in their lives?

When you face God's calling for your life, which is more of a problem for you: pride or timidity? What steps can you take to fully surrender to his leading? How would it affect what you think, say, and do?

Father, I follow you because you are worthy. Today, I surrender to you and I trust you to...

Joshua and Caleb
THE BATTLE TEST

> Joshua son of Nun and Caleb son of Jephunneh, who were among those who had explored the land, tore their clothes and said to the entire Israelite assembly, "The land we passed through and explored is exceedingly good. If the Lord is pleased with us, he will lead us into that land, a land flowing with milk and honey, and will give it to us. Only do not rebel against the Lord. And do not be afraid of the people of the land, because we will swallow them up. Their protection is gone, but the Lord is with us. Do not be afraid of them." (Numbers 14:6-9)

I'm not sure where the thought came from, but some Christians to-day believe that God is (or at least he *should* be) devoted to making our lives as pleasant as possible. I've heard pastors promise a carefree, "effortless" life, full of pleasures and devoid of any difficulties. When I read the Scriptures and look at the lives of faithful men and women throughout history, however, I see something much different. Without exception, they faced difficulties, trials, suffering, and heartache. Their faith grew strong in the hot fires of struggle and on the anvil of accusation and temptation—not because God protected them from hardships. Throughout the Bible, the writers describe fierce combat as part of a life of faith. As Paul described in his letter to the Ephesians, sometimes our "struggle is not against flesh and blood, but against the rulers, against the authorities, against the powers of this dark world and against the spiritual forces of evil in the heavenly realms" (Ephesians 6:12). Sometimes, though, we read about God's people engaging in physical warfare, especially in the Old Testament.

When Moses led the people out of Egypt, he prepared them to enter the Promised Land, a land full of abundant resources. The Scriptures even say it was "flowing with milk and honey"! Moses sent a dozen spies to look at the land and report what it would take to conquer it. When the spies returned after looking at Canaan, the majority told of giants who couldn't be defeated. They warned of tragedy and death if God's people proceeded. But two members of this Special Forces Op, Joshua and Caleb, brought back a different report. Would it be difficult to conquer? Sure it would, but God had just defeated the pharaoh's army, the most powerful military force in the world. And God had used miraculous powers to free them from slavery. Why would they doubt his strength now? The greatness of their God, the two men assured Moses and the people, was more than a match for the military strength of the nations occupying Canaan.

But the people chose the majority report. They could have entered the land in a couple of weeks, but because they were faithless, the people wandered in the desert for another 40 years. By then, the entire generation had died—all except the two men whose faith had given them courage to fight when others cowered in fear. Even Moses died before he reached the land promised by God. In his place, God picked a new leader, Joshua. Again, God performed miracles, stopping the flow of the Jordan so the people could cross and causing the collapse of the walls of Jericho in their first military victory, but the conquest of the land wouldn't be won in bloodless battles. Men would fight and die to receive the promise. Joshua led the army, but Caleb wasn't far behind. Now an old man, he looked at the hill country full of the fiercest native warriors and exclaimed boldly, "Give me that mountain!" We need more like him today.

My good friend Jackson Senyonga is the pastor of one of the largest churches in the world. He planted his 40,000-member church in Kapala,

Uganda in 1997 with a tent revival meeting. Hundreds of people were coming to Christ, being healed, and finding deliverance from bondage — causing a major economic crisis for the local witchdoctors who were losing business. In the second week of meetings, the head witchdoctor in town walked into their service and announced to everyone that he was giving Pastor Jackson three days to quit preaching and tear down his tent or Pastor Jackson would surely die. Filled with righteous indignation, Pastor Jackson turned to him in front of the crowd and pronounced that he could repent of his sin and turn to the one true God, or the curse he has spoken would come back on him.

This was a cosmic showdown, much like the days of Elijah on Mount Carmel. For two days the meetings went on and people were saved. On the morning of the third day the witchdoctor came to the church and asked Jackson why he wasn't dead. He asked, "What power do you have working on your behalf?" Jackson told him about Jesus Christ, the one true God of heaven who died on the cross and rose from the grave. The witchdoctor asked him if this God could save him from the demons that were tormenting him. Jackson said, "My God is big enough to save me and you both. All you have to do is surrender your life to him."

The witchdoctor not only got saved, but he is now a church planter. Under the direction of Pastor Jackson, the whole congregation went with the witchdoctor to the Temples of Satan in the town and burned them down. Thousands of people came out to see the spectacle, fully expecting for the Christians to die where they stood. After the temples burned down, people realized they were finally free from Satan's grip on them. There was great worship and shouting in the city, and thousands of people came to know Christ. In this African town and in our lives, too, God will always give us the victory, but that doesn't mean it will be without a fight.

Even with God's clear promises, we can expect conflict. If we think God's presence guarantees smooth sailing, we'll be deeply confused and disappointed when we encounter difficulties along the way. We will think that God has let us down, and we may conclude that he has completely abandoned us. Our test in these situations is to trust that God will give us the wisdom, strength, and "kingdom eyes" we need to fight and win—no matter how long it takes.

We need to see the world around us with spiritual eyes. God has given us many things to enjoy, and countless blessings fill our lives, but we live in a world of evil spiritual forces. If we aren't aware of them, we'll be shocked when we encounter their attacks and roadblocks. But we also need to remember that God is greater—*far* greater—than any enemy forces in our world. We can trust him to work in us and through us to defeat them.

Quite often, the battle is won or lost before the fighting begins. It all depends on our expectations. Entitlement isn't just a word used to describe government social programs; it permeates our entire culture with the attitude that says, "I deserve my life to be easy, fun, and successful." When believers have this attitude, it robs us of tenacity, perspective, and daily victory because our unfulfilled expectations create too much self-pity and resentment to fight effectively. In contrast, we need to realize that God uses the fight to develop our faith. Author and professor J. I. Packer offers this insight about God's purpose for putting us in the middle of spiritual battle:

> "This is what all the work of grace aims at—an even deeper knowledge of God, and an ever closer fellowship with Him. Grace is God drawing us sinners closer and closer to Him. How does God in grace prosecute this purpose? Not by shielding us from assault by the world, the flesh, and the devil, nor by protecting us from burdensome and frustrating circumstances, nor yet by shielding us from troubles created by our own temperament and psychology; but rather by exposing us to all these things, so as to overwhelm us with a sense of our own inadequacy, and to drive us to cling to Him more closely. This is the ultimate reason,

from our standpoint, why God fills our lives with troubles and perplexities of one sort or another—it is to ensure that we shall learn to hold Him fast."[6]

What is the fight for you and me? Most of us don't actively fight against foreign armies that attack us with guns and grenades. Our enemies are much closer to home. The forces we fight against are temptation, jealousy, self-pity, and greed of every sort. We struggle with paying bills, but the real fight is living within our means. We fight to carve out a sense of purpose in life, but we waste a lot of time daydreaming about having the perfect lifestyle. Parents enter the battle each day to trust God for direction in raising their children to have godly values and live for Christ. When a 16-year-old daughter gets pregnant, do we give up and walk away from her, or do we stay in the struggle to support her? Do we fight against her or for her? We face conflicts against sickness, death, broken relationships, disappointing careers, and discouragement of every stripe.

Sometimes, the battle we face is internal instead of external. When Joshua led his men against the little town of Ai, they lost the fight because someone in their camp had disobeyed God. Joshua tore his clothes and cried out to God, and he told Joshua to clean up his own people before he went out to battle again.

Thankfully, God gives us a miracle like Jericho from time to time, but far more often, he asks us to strap on our swords, pick up our shields, and courageously enter the battle. Like Joshua, Caleb, and the Israelite army, we will get bloody, and it will take a lot of effort, but we'll see God work all along the way. When this happens, we see a miracle there, too—the miracle of men and women staying faithful to God in the midst of conflict in their lives.

---

6 Packer, *Knowing God*, p. 227.

How does a sense of entitlement ("I deserve more") erode our courage in tough times?

In what way is the real battle in our minds before we ever take action in spiritual battle?

In what area of your life do you need to be more courageous like Joshua and Caleb? What steps can you take today in that area?

Almighty God, I want to be courageous in battle. Help me...

Samson
THE SUBMISSION TEST

His father and mother replied, "Isn't there an acceptable woman among your relatives or among all our people? Must you go to the uncircumcised Philistines to get a wife?" But Samson said to his father, "Get her for me. She's the right one for me." (Judges 14:3)

Nothing is more attractive than manly strength under the control and direction of God, and nothing is more beautiful than a woman who loves God with all her heart. Hormones are powerful forces in our lives—not just in the bodies of teenagers, but to some degree for all of us. The story of Samson shows how this power can become terribly destructive. Again and again, Samson fails to submit his testosterone to God.

Samson's birth foreshadowed another child's entrance into the world centuries later. Like the angel's encounter with Mary, the angel of the Lord came to Samson's parents and announced the birth of a special child. Both Samson and Jesus were appointed as servants, but only one fulfilled God's intention. In the first scene of Samson as a young man, he insisted on marrying a Philistine woman against the expressed wishes of his parents. On his way to the wedding, he passed by a dead lion with a hive of bees inside making honey. To entertain his wife's 30 guests, he made a bet with them: If they could guess the answer to a riddle, he'd give them fine clothes. For days, the men labored to figure out the answer, but it proved impossible. Finally, they pressured Samson's wife. She begged him to give her the answer, and when he refused, she wept long and hard. Samson isn't the first man to give in to his wife's tearful demands, but that's no excuse. Doing what's convenient to appease a spouse proved destructive for him, just as it is for us. He told her the secret, and she told her friends. To pay his debt, Samson killed 30 men and took their clothes. Enraged, he stomped off, leaving his new bride to his best man. Some would say that he proved his strength by killing so many men, but he miserably failed the test of godly manhood.

Samson's life was checkered with victories and defeats, tests passed and tests failed. The next scene in the biblical narrative is during the harvest season when Samson tried to visit the wife he had abandoned only months before. Her father refused to let him see her, but he offered Samson her younger sister. Again, Samson's anger burned. To get revenge, he tied the tails of 300 foxes together, two by two, and set them on fire. When they ran through the Philistine grain fields, the harvest of grain, grapes, and olives was destroyed. The Philistines (sweet people all) burned his wife and her father to death. The cycle of revenge continued with Samson killing many men.

The Philistines came to Judah and insisted that the people turn Samson over to them. They meekly complied, but God's Spirit gave Samson incredible strength, and he killed a thousand men with the jawbone of a donkey! Why would God empower and use a tragically flawed man like Samson? Simply because that's all the raw material he has in us humans. We're all flawed to some degree. To his credit, Samson was willing for God to use him to free his people from Philistine oppression.

But the tests weren't over for Samson. After a night with a prostitute (yet another failed test of submission to God's will), he fell in love with Delilah, another Philistine woman. The Philistine rulers offered her a lot of money if she could uncover the secret of his great strength. For several days, she tried to trick him into giving up this information, but each time, he refused. She begged and threatened him day after day. "Then she said to him, 'How can you say, "I love you," when you won't confide in me? This is the third time you have made a fool of me and haven't told me the secret of your great strength.' With such nagging she prodded him day after day until he was tired to death" (Judges 16:15-16).

When Samson couldn't take it any longer, he told her the secret: "It's in the hair, babe." She told the Philistine rulers, and that night when he was asleep, she cut his hair. Without his strength, they easily captured him, tore out his eyes, and put him in heavy chains. Again, giving in to this woman only caused more trouble. He had failed the same test again.

The Philistines mocked their captured enemy, but Samson's hair began to grow. During a big celebration, Samson found one more way to let his hormones dictate his life. As they made fun of him at the party, he grabbed the center pillars and pulled with all his might. The building collapsed on them—and him, killing more in his death than during his violent life.

Humility isn't wimpiness or shying away from taking initiative. It's strength under control. God gave Samson great strength, but too often, he used it for selfish purposes: for sex, to intimidate, to marry a foreign woman (or two), and to get revenge at every turn. Beauty and feminine wiles can be used just as powerfully as male testosterone to manipulate people. All of us have God-given abilities, resources, and strengths. The question is whether we'll let our hormones rule us, or if we'll submit every aspect of our lives—including our drives and desires—to God. Demanding our own way eventually leads to destruction. Hormone-driven men use women instead of loving them, they always have to win at every endeavor, and they lose their cool whenever anybody or anything gets in the way. Women whose lives are directed by their hormones live to seduce men, feel terribly jealous when perceived rivals vie for their men's affections, and compare themselves with every other woman they see. For men and women, living this way keeps them in perpetual adolescence. Wise men and women recognize the benefits of humility and learn to live beyond their hormones.

When my little brother Dallas was just a little boy, he went through "the terrible twos," but that stage lasted through the threes and fours. He was awful! He demanded his own way at every turn, and he pitched a fit if he didn't get what he wanted immediately. (I remember my mother shaking her head and wondering out loud if he was possessed!) No amount of pleading, explaining, or spanking seemed to make a dent in the young boy's life.

One night, Dallas walked over to the refrigerator and told my dad, "I want a soda."

Dad looked him in the eye and said, "No, Dallas. It's too late."

Dallas opened the refrigerator and grabbed a can. He turned and looked at Dad in abject defiance.

Dad got up and walked toward him. He took the can from my brother, spanked his hand, and put the can back in the refrigerator.

Dallas stood there for a few seconds, and then he opened the refrigerator and took the can out again. But now he was screaming and crying in his anger at my dad.

Again, Dad took the can from him and put it back. Dad spanked him and told him, "Son, I told you 'no' and I meant 'no.' " This tug of war went on for about 15 minutes, but it seemed like hours. Dad later told me that he realized this moment was going to prove to be pivotal in Dallas' life. No matter how much he begged, pleaded, and threatened, Dad simply couldn't let him get away with disobedience.

I wish I could say that this was the turning point in Dallas' life, but it wasn't. He continued to be an obstinate child for several more years. When he was about six, he disobeyed my mother for the 428,498th time. She said, "Son, go to your room. You're going to get a spanking." She paused for a long moment and then sighed deeply, "Son, I don't know why you keep being so disobedient. It just doesn't make sense to me."

He went into his bedroom, and a few minutes later, Mom walked in. For some reason, he looked up at her and said, "Mom, let's just talk." Ordinarily, Mom might think this was a thinly veiled ploy of a child trying to get out of a spanking, but she could sense that this moment was different. For the first time in his life, Dallas wanted to live by reason, not instinct. From that day, he never got another spanking because he was willing to listen to reason, to resolve problems, and find solutions. It was the turning point my parents had prayed about for many years, and it was glorious—for all of us.

Our human instincts and hormones are powerful drives, but they often lead to destructive and painful consequences. Early in our lives, some of us learn to live above them by reason and the Spirit of God, but for a few people, that breakthrough never comes. It never came for Samson. Even in his last days, when he was a blind, mocked prisoner, rage controlled his life. We become wise, not because we don't have powerful hormones, but when we put them under the control of God's Spirit.

Describe the attractiveness of a strong man who is humble and of a beautiful woman who lives for God.

What are some keys to living in submission to God's plans instead of by hormone-driven desires?

Have you come to that turning point? Explain your answer.

Father, I don't want to be like Samson because...

Eli and His Sons
THE IMAGE MANAGEMENT TEST

> Now Eli, who was very old, heard about everything his sons were doing to all Israel and how they slept with the women who served at the entrance to the Tent of Meeting. So he said to them, "Why do you do such things? I hear from all the people about these wicked deeds of yours. No, my sons; it is not a good report that I hear spreading among the Lord's people." (1 Samuel 2:22-24)

We live in a world where images seem more important than substance. Many of the celebrities searched most often online aren't famous for their great acts of service; they're famous only for being famous. It didn't use to be that way. Only a generation ago, we valued heroism. In his book, *The Greatest Generation,* Tom Brokaw shined a spotlight on men and women who sacrificed themselves for others. They gave, bled, and died so others could live in freedom. Today, though, people in our culture value comfort, affluence, and making sure we look good to people around us. Too often, we expect (and, in fact, demand) to be praised even when our hearts are rotten. When we don't get the acclaim we insist on getting, we complain bitterly, seldom looking beneath the surface to deal with the interior issues of the heart.

Though it certainly isn't the only cause for our lofty expectations, advertising has had a powerful impact on us. The purpose of advertising is to create discontent so that people will hope a product or service will fulfill their desires. In his book, *The Technological Society,* French cultural analyst Jacques Ellul observed,

> "One of the great designs of advertising is to create needs; but this is possible only if these needs correspond to an ideal of life that man accepts. The way of life offered by advertising is all the more compelling in that it corresponds to certain easy and simple tendencies of man and refers to a world in which there are no spiritual values to form and inform life. When men feel and respond to the needs advertising creates, they are adhering to its ideal of life. The human tendencies upon which advertising like this is based may be strikingly simpleminded, but they nonetheless represent pretty much the level of our modern life. Advertising offers us the ideal we have always wanted (and that ideal is certainly not a heroic way of life)."[7]

Ellul's insights are brilliant and piercing. The "ideal" life depicted in modern advertising promises to fulfill our expectations of wealth, ease, happiness, and a consistently positive image, no matter the actual condition of our character. In stark contrast, the "heroic" life is one of honor, duty, sacrifice, and joyful service to others. Why do we focus so much on our image? Dale Carnegie stated succinctly, "We are creatures of emotion, bristling with prejudice and motivated by pride and vanity." Selfishness crowds out heroism.

Eli was a priest in God's temple in Jerusalem, but having a high position certainly doesn't guarantee a person's integrity. British Lord Acton famously said, "Power corrupts, and absolute power corrupts

---

7   jan.ucc.nau.edu/~jsa3/hum355/readings/ellul.htm

absolutely." Eli was a corrupt man, and we see his selfishness and cowardice clearly in his relationship with his sons. They were awful. It's hard to put into words how despicably they acted. They were commissioned by God to protect and serve his people, but Eli's sons sexually assaulted women, stole from men, and mocked them all. Rumors spread throughout God's people that these men couldn't be trusted. Soon, other reports corroborated the news about them, and the city buzzed with accusations.

Any good and noble father would have taken action at the first suspicion of this kind of behavior from his kids, but not Eli. He let it go on and on, saying, in effect, "Boys will be boys!" Then people started talking about him, accusing him of being a terrible father. Well, this was different. It was all right for people to say ugly things about the boys, but now it was time to correct his crumbling image. The old man confronted his sons, but his motivation for change wasn't to honor God or even to avoid consequences for their sin—it was to make himself look better in the eyes of people.

The Scriptures give us many layers of motivation to live for God and make good decisions. Some are practical. The law of the harvest promises that we will reap *what* we sow, *after* we sow, and *more than* we sow. Ultimately, pleasing God outranks all other motives. When Jesus taught about the kingdom, John tells us that some people wanted to follow him but were intimidated by the Pharisees. John's conclusion was that "they loved praise from men more than praise from God" (John 12:43). Public displays of righteousness designed to impress others don't impress God at all. In his most famous sermon, Jesus told his followers, "Be careful not to do your 'acts of righteousness' before men, to be seen by them. If you do, you will have no reward from your Father in heaven" (Matthew 6:1). To make sure they understood, he told them to pray in secret, give without letting others know how much you're giving, and fast without telling anyone. Jesus assures us that God knows our hearts, and he will reward us if we don't engage in image management to show others how righteous we are.

All of us are tempted to give more attention to the externals people see, rather than the internals only God sees, but maturity involves focusing our attention on what matters most to God. When I was a boy, I was a PK, a preacher's kid, and everybody let me know it all day every day. I hated that label because it created unrealistic expectations for a boy trying to find himself. On a Career Day in school one year, some friends and I sneaked out and went to the donut shop. While we were paying, a man recognized me and said, "Shouldn't you be in school?"

I nodded and said we were going there right now. That wasn't good enough for him. He shook his head and scowled, "Sneaking out of school. I would have never suspected this from you, being a preacher's kid and all!"

To my Mom's great credit, when I told her about the man's comment, she didn't think about her own image at all. She said, "Son, you shouldn't do what's right because you're a preacher's kid. You should do the right thing because you're God's kid." I've known Christian leaders who put a lot of pressure on their children to act a certain way, but my parents never did that to us. My parents cared about their sons walking with God. Period. How we looked in other people's eyes wasn't even on the radar. They never compared us to other people's kids, and they never saw our behavior as a tool to dull or sharpen their own reputations. Their perspective gave me a lot of freedom and security, and it motivated me to do the right thing to honor them and the Lord. I can never thank them enough.

Labels and expectations can get us off track. If we value only what others think of us and say about us, we'll try to manage our images like it's a big game. But aligning our hearts with God's purposes isn't a game. It's life, breath, joy, and peace. God cares not only about our reputations, but even more, how we earn our reputations. He looks into the secret places of our hearts to see if we're truly honest with him and with ourselves. Brutal honesty is necessary if we're going to avoid Eli's shallow motive of managing his public image. When we're honest with God, he can change us from the inside out, and that's when we learn to be real heroes who serve selflessly and boldly for God's sake. God treasures true repentance and righteousness, not the phony kind that only cares about what others think of us.

What are some differences between celebrities and real heroes?

What are some ways people (maybe even you) try to manage their public image? What are the results?

What is one thing you can do today in secret to worship God or serve others, to combat the desire in each of us to be recognized?

Father, I want to love you and serve you from the depths of my soul. Today, help me to...

Samuel
THE THIN SKIN TEST

So all the elders of Israel gathered together and came to Samuel at Ramah. They said to him, "You are old, and your sons do not walk in your ways; now appoint a king to lead us, such as all the other nations have." But when they said, "Give us a king to lead us," this displeased Samuel; so he prayed to the Lord. And the Lord told him: "Listen to all that the people are saying to you; it is not you they have rejected, but they have rejected me as their king." (1 Samuel 8:4-7)

Nobody likes to be overlooked or taken for granted. It hurts, and for some of us, it's devastating. In the Christian world, we want to be perceived as humble, effective servants—but we sure don't want to be treated like a servant! Some people have very thick skins. Nothing, it seems, gets to them. (In fact, some of them are clueless about how others perceive them, and they don't really care.) But most of us live at the other end of the spectrum. We care too much about what others think of us. We have very thin skins, and we get hurt very easily. All it takes is a word, or maybe just a sideways glance or rolling eyes to make us feel insignificant.

There's nothing wrong with wanting to feel loved, accepted, and valued. That's human nature, and God has gone to great lengths to assure us that we're incredibly important to him. He has proven his love by the ultimate demonstration of his affection: Christ's death on the cross for us. The Scriptures assure us that he's thinking about us and praying for us all the time. The problem is that we value the fickle approval of "flesh and blood" folks around us more than the rock-solid love of God.

We're not alone in this struggle. The prophet Samuel was in the same boat. He had served faithfully for many years by leading the nation as God's representative, but the people were tired of the government God had given them. They looked around at the other nations ruled by kings, and they wanted a king, too. In a dig that must have hurt, they didn't just say, "We want a king." They told Samuel, "You're old, and you haven't been a good enough father so that we trust your sons to rule us. We like the idea of a king, so we want you to appoint one for us."

How would you have felt? We probably would have been hurt and angry, and we might have stomped off and said something like, "Oh yeah, well, you'll be sorry! I'll get you a king, but before long, you'll wish I was still God's prophet over you." A couple of us may have even stuck our tongues out at them!

To thicken our skin a bit, we need to do a few things. First, we need to realize that people make their own choices, and we shouldn't always take those choices personally. Sometimes it's a direct offense to us, but quite often, their decision has nothing to do with us personally. God told Samuel, "They haven't rejected you, but they've rejected me." In the same way, often people aren't really saying "no" to us, but they're saying "no" to God and his will for their lives. We just happen to be standing as God's spokesman at the moment.

Second, God is the source of our value and self-concept, and his love never fails. Even when we've blown it, he still loves us, forgives us, and gives us another chance. When we're feeling overlooked, we can be sure that the God of the universe never forgets about us. In a beautiful, poetic image, Isaiah tells us that we're inscribed on the palms of his hands (Isaiah 49:16).

Third, we need to forgive those who hurt us. We tend to make one of two mistakes in forgiveness: we either forgive too quickly or too late. Some of us want to get the conflict and the bad feelings over with as soon as possible, and we want to be conscientious Christians, so we say, "Oh, it doesn't matter. I forgive you. Now let's forget about it and move on." But it *does* matter. When we feel genuinely hurt, we've lost something meaningful to us. In these cases, forgiveness must always be accompanied by a measure of grief over our sense of loss. We have to be honest about the hurt so that we can truly forgive the offender.

When we refuse to forgive, we hurt ourselves far more than we hurt the other person. Why do we hold on to resentment? Why do we let anger fester into bitterness? Those angry emotions give us two things that we perceive as benefits: identity and energy. As long as we can play the role of the victim, we are "the one who was wronged," and we can blame our self-absorbed behavior on someone else. Bitterness also gives us an adrenaline rush. We wake up every day thinking of ways we can get back at that person who hurt us. Author and pastor Frederick Buechner described the bitter person's reason to live and the consequences of harboring this resentment:

> "Of the Seven Deadly Sins, anger is possibly the most fun. To lick your wounds, to smack your lips over grievances long past, to roll over your tongue the prospect of bitter confrontations still to come, to savor to the last toothsome morsel both the pain you are given and the pain you are giving back—in many ways it is a feast fit for a king. The chief drawback is that what you are wolfing down is yourself. The skeleton at the feast is you!"[8]

For some of us, our thin skin began long ago in homes where we didn't feel safe and loved. Now, almost any slight seems like an atomic bomb devastating us! And some of us are in relationships at home and at

---

8   Frederick Buechner, *Wishful Thinking,* (Harper San Francisco, 1993), p. 2.

work with people who seem to get a kick out of demeaning us day after day. They may say enough nice things to keep us off guard, but they know how to throw those zingers that pierce our hearts. Forgiveness means that we release a person from a debt and refuse to take revenge, but it doesn't mean we have to trust someone who has proven to be untrustworthy. Healing wounds takes time, and we need to find a safe, healthy environment where we can learn to forgive, grieve, and grow.

Years ago, my Dad did some business with a man near our home. At first, they had a very good relationship, or at least it seemed that way. After Dad paid him for some work to be done, the man dragged his feet. Dad called him over and over again, but he didn't do the work. The amount of money was substantial, and after a while, the monetary loss began to hurt our family. Over several months, I watched the relational and financial strain take its toll on my Dad. The problem was never resolved. Years later when we built the church in Red Oak, I realized that I had to drive past this guy's office going to and from work each day. Dad seemed to have been able to forgive him, but I couldn't. Every time I drove by, my anger burned. Early one morning after months of torment, I prayed, "Lord, this man really hurt my Dad and our family. I know you want me to forgive him, but I just can't."

At that moment, God spoke to my heart: "I've given you a process to forgive him. Every time you drive by, make a commitment to let go of the anger and refuse to take revenge. In time, your feelings will catch up to your choice to forgive."

Starting that day, every time I passed his office, I raised my hand and said, "God, bless that man. I forgive him. Lord, bless his family and his business. Everything I ask you to do for me and my family, I ask you to do for him."

Change didn't happen quickly, but it happened. The rock of bitterness in my heart required a lot of chipping away, but after three years of praying God's blessing on him twice a day, my perspective changed completely. By then, I genuinely loved him and wanted God's best for him. My statements each day were no longer just words. They were heartfelt convictions. I'm really glad that God worked in my heart because three years after I began praying for him, I found myself on a committee with him. He and I spent two hours each month sitting at the same table! And we became friends. God had given me the capacity to forgive and to love in a way I never knew was possible. Some people laugh or wince when I tell them it took three years, but that's okay. No matter how much time it took, it was worth it. (Early in the process of my transformation, Dad made an appointment with him and went to see him. Dad chose to forgive him and was free from resentment and bitterness. It took me a little longer!)

The Christian life isn't just about managing our anger and not exploding at those who offend us. It's a lot richer and deeper than that. Paul tells us to forgive others "just as God in Christ has forgiven us." In other words, we can only express as much forgiveness as we've experienced. If we're having a hard time forgiving someone, our first step is to drink deeply from the well of God's great mercy toward us. Then, with full hearts, we'll be able to forgive those who have hurt us. But don't expect to feel warm and fuzzy. Forgiveness is first a choice. Then, after a while, our emotions catch up to our decision.

I think we are most like Christ when we choose to forgive those who offend us. And the world is watching. Jesus told his followers, "You have heard that it was said, 'Love your neighbor and hate your enemy.' But I tell you: Love your enemies and pray for those who persecute you, that you may be sons of your Father in heaven" (Matthew 6:43-45).

Are you a bit too thin-skinned? If you are, try not to take others' choices too personally, drink deeply of God's infinite love for you, and learn the fine art of forgiveness.

What are some ways thin-skinned people react to those who hurt them?

Why do we tend to take other's choices personally?

In what area(s) of your life are you thin-skinned? (Is it a recurring situation or a person?) How can you apply each of the three elements of "skin-thickening" to your situation?

Reflect on the elements of forgiveness in today's lesson. Which point stands out to you? What, if anything, do you need to do to forgive someone who has hurt you?

Jesus, thank you for forgiving me. I want to follow your example by...

Saul
THE OBEDIENCE TEST

When Samuel reached him, Saul said, "The Lord bless you! I have carried out the Lord's instructions."

But Samuel said, "What then is this bleating of sheep in my ears? What is this lowing of cattle that I hear?" (1 Samuel 15:13-14)

We live in a "no-fault" society where people don't want to take responsibility for their choices. We have no-fault auto insurance, no-fault divorce, and no-fault relationships of every kind. When someone presses us to take responsibility for our decisions, many people just shrug and walk away. The problem of not owning our decisions, though, isn't new. It's as old as time. When Adam and Eve tragically sinned, God confronted Adam and he replied, "The woman you gave me made me do it!" In one sentence, Adam blamed both Eve and God for his sin. Pretty slick, don't you think? We've been copying him ever since.

When the people of God asked for a king so they could be like other nations, God relented and gave them one. Saul was the tallest, most handsome man in the land, but good looks and a promotion don't guarantee integrity. His brief reign on the throne was a string of disasters.

Twice, he knew what God wanted him to do, blew it, and then used excuses or blamed somebody else.

In those days, the chief antagonists of the Israelites were the Philistines. One of Saul's earliest actions was to attack and defeat the Philistine outpost of Geba. This victory, though, didn't bring peace to Israel; it made the Philistines furious, and they plotted revenge. As they approached, Saul's army became terrified and fell apart. Some fled, and some hid in caves, behind bushes, and under rocks. The king and the few men who remained with him shook with fear. Samuel, God's representative, had promised to come, but day after day passed for Saul and his dwindling army in front of the Philistine hordes. The king's fear matched his desperation. He decided to take matters into his own hands and perform a priestly act of offering a sacrifice to God. Most of us can't really grasp the significance of this act because we aren't familiar with the clear delineation of roles in Israel: Priests offer sacrifices; kings rule the nation. Saul's timing was, as always for him, terrible. As soon as he finished, Samuel walked up.

"What have you done?" the old man asked.

The king responded with a studied display of blame shifting. First, he offered a practical rationalization for his behavior: "The soldiers were leaving." If he offered a sacrifice to get God's blessing, he thought they'd stay. Then he blamed Samuel: "And you weren't here when you said you'd be." (King Saul must have missed the point that Samuel was standing right in front of him.)

The old prophet, though, didn't buy the excuse or accept the blame. He retorted, "You acted foolishly! You haven't obeyed the command of the Lord your God." No wiggle room there.

Saul's second colossal failure to obey occurred a short time later. This time, God's instructions were crystal clear. "Samuel said to Saul, 'I am the one the Lord sent to anoint you king over his people Israel; so listen now to the message from the Lord. This is what the Lord Almighty says: "I will punish the Amalekites for what they did to Israel when they waylaid them as they came up from Egypt. Now go, attack the Amalekites and totally destroy everything that belongs to them. Do not spare them; put to death men and women, children and infants, cattle and sheep, camels and donkeys." ' " (1 Samuel 15:1-3)

Saul attacked the Amalekites, but he was less than thorough in following God's directions. He let King Agag live, and he and the men kept the best sheep, cattle, and lambs. When Samuel went to Saul's camp the next morning, Saul met him with a sunny smile. "Be blessed," he told Samuel. "We did exactly what God commanded!"

"Oh yeah," I can almost hear the plaintive tone in Samuel's voice. "What then is this bleating of sheep in my ears? What is this lowing of cattle that I hear?'"

"Oh that," replied the king. "The soldiers took them to offer sacrifices to God."

Yeah, right. Samuel didn't buy Saul's blame shifting the first time, and he didn't buy it this time either. The king protested and tried to convince the old man, but Samuel knew better.

"But Samuel replied:
 'Does the Lord delight in burnt offerings and sacrifices
 as much as in obeying the voice of the Lord?
 To obey is better than sacrifice,
 and to heed is better than the fat of rams.

For rebellion is like the sin of divination,
 and arrogance like the evil of idolatry.
 Because you have rejected the word of the Lord,
 he has rejected you as king' " (1 Samuel 15:22-23).

It's a tragic story, but before we shake our heads at Saul, we need to ask how well we pass the obedience test. How often do we make excuses for choosing the easy way, and how often do we blame others for our failures? That's the obedience test, and we all fail it from time to time.

In our culture, obedience seems optional to many people. We're glad to follow God as long as we get plenty of benefits and it's not too demanding, but when God asks us to do something we don't want to do, we find convenient excuses. "I didn't have time," "I didn't know how to do that," "She wouldn't help me, so it was too hard," and a dozen more. And sometimes we're like Saul, claiming that we're obedient when we're not.

We live in such a self-absorbed culture that some believers don't know what God has commanded us to be and do. I'm not talking about the special instructions God gives to us sometimes when the Spirit whispers to our hearts. Those, I've found, are often reserved for men and women who have been responsive to the clear directives God has given in his word. A friend of mine asked people in a Bible study to list some of the commands God had given believers. After "love God with all your heart" and "love your neighbor as yourself," silence blanketed the room. My friend told them there are countless commands in the Bible, and many passages with several listed. He asked them to turn to Romans 12, and they read a series of crisp, clear commands: Love sincerely, hate evil, cling to what is good, be devoted to each other in brotherly love, honor others above yourselves, don't lack in zeal, stay enthusiastic, be joyful in hope, patient in affliction, and faithful in prayer. The list continues, but he felt he had made his point. He asked, "How are you doing with these commands?"

A member of the group commented, "Well, I can't say, but now at least I have a starting point."

To pass the obedience test, we first have to have a relationship with the One we are to obey, and then we need to know what he has directed us to do. Without those, we're just wandering in the dark. We can ask God for wisdom and courage to carry out the plans he has given us, and we need to hang out with others who are serious about following him with all their hearts.

All of us wrestle with the temptation to rationalize our disobedience and blame others for our faults. I'm in the people business, and I find out things about people that are highly confidential. Sometimes, I want to tell some juicy news that will make me look superior, but it will come at another person's expense. Gossip, no matter how I try to rationalize or excuse it, is sin. The proverbs warn of the consequences of gossip, and Paul tells us, "Do not let any unwholesome talk come out of your mouths, but only what is helpful for building others up according to their needs, that it may benefit those who listen" (Ephesians 4:29). Those are clear commands for me to obey, and I have to ask myself each day if I'm passing the obedience test.

If the commands of God aren't clear in our minds, we'll fail miserably. Even if we know them, we'll be tempted to find excuses when obedience isn't convenient or when it's scary. And we'll want to blame others when we've failed. Know God, learn his instructions, trust him for courage, and find friends who love God with all their hearts. That will help you pass the obedience test, even when you feel all alone.

When my Mom and Dad moved our family to Dallas, we couldn't sell our house in Austin, and our family experienced some financial difficulties. It was especially frustrating to my mother because she felt we had sacrificially obeyed the Lord in moving, and yet it seemed like God was slow on coming through with the money we needed to make ends meet.

One week, my brother Brent needed $15 to pay for his school lunches, but Mom didn't have the money for it. She could have scraped together some meager sandwiches, or she could have borrowed some money from a friend to make better lunches, but she wanted to trust God for a miracle. She and Brent prayed for God to provide: "God, you are the one who brought us here, so please give us a sign that you're still with us."

As Mom walked Brent to school, they looked on the ground and saw a one-dollar bill. They were thrilled! A few feet away, they found another, and then another. In a few minutes, they found 15 one-dollar bills. The greatest part of that miracle wasn't just that God put the exact amount of money they needed in the right place at the right time, but that God was letting them know that he heard their prayers, saw their need, and was still with them all along the way.

This is the confidence you can have when you walk in obedience to God — he is with you, and he won't let you down.

What are some excuses people (maybe even you) have used to avoid responsibility for disobedience?

What are some specific things you know that God wants you to obey, follow, and do today?

Who is someone who is a good model of joyful obedience to God? Similarly, who is someone who can be a resource to help you pursue obedience to God's commands? How can you enlist that person's help?

Father, give me wisdom and courage today to...

David
THE WAITING TEST

> Saul recognized David's voice and said, "Is that your voice, David my son?" David replied, "Yes it is, my Lord the king." And he added, "Why is my Lord pursuing his servant? What have I done, and what wrong am I guilty of? Now let my Lord the king listen to his servant's words. If the Lord has incited you against me, then may he accept an offering. If, however, men have done it, may they be cursed before the Lord! They have now driven me from my share in the Lord's inheritance and have said, 'Go, serve other gods.' Now do not let my blood fall to the ground far from the presence of the Lord. The king of Israel has come out to look for a flea—as one hunts a partridge in the mountains." (1 Samuel 26:17-20)

When we think of King David, we usually imagine him as the boy who killed Goliath, a mighty king, or his sin of adultery with Bathsheba and the murder of Uriah. Sometimes forgotten in the history of David is the incredible struggle he had between the day he was anointed king and the day he actually took the throne. For a long, long time, David had to wait. To me, his attitude and actions during that time are some of the most remarkable of his life—probably because I hate to wait! But I'm not alone.

Author and pastor Charles Swindoll says that waiting is perhaps the hardest task God asks a Christian to do. We live in an instant society. We use microwaves to cook our food, ATMs to get money, and drive-thrus for fast food and dry cleaning. One of the ways life has changed for many of us is that we expect to stay connected to everyone and everything through our cell phones, PDAs, text messaging, email, and the Internet. We can hardly have a conversation without stopping to take a call or read a message. Linda Stone, formerly of Apple and Microsoft, coined the term "continuous partial attention" to describe the constant distractions of our communication devices. She reports:

"To pay continuous partial attention is to pay partial attention— CONTINUOUSLY. It is motivated by a desire to be a LIVE node on the network. Another way of saying this is that we want to connect and be connected. We want to effectively scan for opportunity and optimize for the best opportunities, activities, and contacts, in any given moment. To be busy, to be connected, is to be alive, to be recognized, and to matter. We pay continuous partial attention in an effort NOT TO MISS ANYTHING. It is an always-on, anywhere, anytime, any place behavior that involves an artificial sense of constant crisis. We are always in high alert when we pay continuous partial attention. This artificial sense of constant crisis is more typical of continuous partial attention than it is of multi-tasking."[9]

Does this always rushed, "always-on" lifestyle have an impact on our willingness to wait on God? You bet it does! We expect him to be as instantaneous as our other communications, but he doesn't want to jump through our hoops. Pastor Jackson Senyonga pastors a church in Uganda. He preached for me recently and said, "Many Christians in America want a 'drive thru' revival—they want it *now*, they want it *big* (supersized), and they want it *cheap* (on the dollar menu)." But is that really how God works with us most of the time?

---

9   www.lindastone.net

David didn't place demands on God to act quickly. After Samuel anointed him as the next king of Israel, David had a small problem: There was already a king in place. Saul was on the throne, and he wasn't even sick! If I had been in David's sandals, I would have been watching for Saul to sneeze. And if I'd had a chance to squeeze him out, I would have taken it. After all, David could have concluded that God's prophet had chosen him, and he probably felt he could do a lot better job than Saul was doing.

A series of events shows David's amazing faith in God's timing. First, the day he was anointed king, David went back to the fields to tend the flock of sheep. He didn't demand power or the throne! Then, Saul and his army were in deep trouble facing the Philistines and their giant. David, the shepherd boy, rose to the occasion and killed Goliath. Saul asked him to serve in his palace and play a harp to soothe his spirit, but the king turned on David and tried to kill him. David fled to the desert, and outlaws from all across the land joined him. Day after day, Saul sent his army to kill David and his "mighty men," but David's skills and God's protection enabled him to escape. One time, David and some of his men were hiding in a cave when Saul came in to go to the bathroom. David crept near him and cut off a corner of his robe. When Saul had left and walked a good distance away, David came out of the cave and yelled to the king, "See the corner of your robe? Now you know I could have killed you, and you have nothing to fear from me." Saul said he was sorry, but he quickly changed his mind and kept up the chase.

During a series of chases that would rival *The Bourne Identity*, David and his men occasionally had to fight against Israel's enemies to protect God's people. Then, when Saul chased him again in the Desert of Ziph, David and Abishai sneaked into the king's camp in the middle of the night and walked right up to Saul. Abishai raised his spear and asked David if he could kill the king, but David again refused to hurt him. Instead, they took Saul's spear and the jug of water that was near him, and they sneaked back to their lines outside the camp. David and his men stood on a hill and shouted to get Saul's attention. David showed Saul the spear and jug in his hands, and he again reminded him that he could have easily killed him. David yelled, "As surely as I valued your life today, so may the Lord value my life and deliver me from all trouble" (1 Samuel 26:24).

Saul again said he was sorry, but he didn't really repent. David had to live with the Philistines and wage war against the Amalekites without the support of the king and his army. Finally, Saul was killed in battle, and David became king. During all this time, David had plenty of opportunities to hurry the process along by killing Saul, and he had lots of chances to complain and feel sorry for himself because it was all so unfair. He didn't do either of these. He was honest about his struggles, but he didn't blame God or take matters into his own hands. Through it all, he trusted God to provide and protect him and his men. He was confident that God would accomplish his will in his way in his timing.

We may be in a hurry, but God never is. He uses delays to test our resolve, purify our hearts, and deepen our trust in him. Time after time, I've seen God use waiting to prepare me, to prepare others around me, or to prepare the elements of a situation. In fact, waiting on God isn't really about time at all—it's about deepening our trust that God will be himself and accomplish what he wants to accomplish. Our task is to be hopeful and expectant as we wait.

When I think of someone who waited patiently with power and grace, I think of Ben Dial, a high school football coach. Coach Dial may have wanted to hear the phone ring with an offer to coach after his NFL career, but he never seemed discontented or hurried. Instead, he poured his heart into the lives of his young players. Year after year, he was more of a life coach than a football coach. He helped them with their schoolwork and their family problems, and he even gave them advice about their girlfriends. For seven years, he invited me to speak at their chapel services. He told them, "Coach Scott is here to coach our spirits." Like David in the wilderness with his mighty men, Coach Dial led these guys with skill and integrity.

One day, Coach Dial's son called to tell me Coach had died from a heart attack on one of the high school fields. When I arrived at the school, I saw about 300 students standing and sitting in the parking lot. They were stunned and crying. Some of the football players came up to me and asked what they should do. I sent them to gather students, and hundreds met at the 50-yard line of the football field. I told them, "Guys, Coach Dial is in the presence of God right now. He wants you to know that he's not just all right—he's fantastic! He told you about his relationship with Christ, and he wants you to know him, too." They asked me to preach at the funeral and at a celebration service at the football field. It was my privilege to honor a man who touched so many lives. In life and in death, Coach Dial was like David, patiently waiting, but using the time to prepare himself and prepare others to be ready. It took five different funeral services to bury Coach Dial. Thousands came to pay their respect, and in all, over 2000 people surrendered their lives to Christ because of his faithful testimony.

As I preached at Coach Dial's funeral services, God worked in powerful ways to use his life and his death to point people to Christ, and I reflected often about the incredible privilege Coach had given me to speak to his players. For seven years, he invited me to conduct the team's devotions before every game. My interactions with players and coaches enabled me to build relationships, and when I spoke in the team's devotions and at the funeral, they knew me and trusted me. To be honest, there were a few times in those seven years that I wanted to stay home or do something else besides drive to the field house and talk about God again. After all, Fridays were my days off, but I felt compelled to go. God used my (sometimes reluctant) readiness to follow him and serve Coach Dial and his team as a foundation to build trust with people, and when Coach died, I had the honor of telling the whole community about his faith and his future with the Savior.

As we see in David's life, times of waiting don't necessarily mean we become passive. David fought for his life, ran like crazy, and built a

Special Forces unit of the toughest guys in the land. Passive? Not in the least. In the same way, our times of waiting certainly include attentive listening to God, but quite often, he wants us to be active in learning new skills, enlisting others to join us, preparing for the next steps, and uncovering resources to use when the time is right.

What are some reasons it's so hard to wait?

What are some ways people respond when they have to wait?

How have you seen God use times of waiting to prepare you, prepare others, or arrange situations so that his blessing is most profound?

What area in your life do you feel like you are in a waiting period? What can you do to make the most of this season in your life? Who can help you?

Father, when you want me to wait, help me to...

Solomon
THE CONTENTMENT
TEST

And I saw that all labor and all achievement spring from man's envy of his neighbor. This too is meaningless, a chasing after the wind. The fool folds his hands and ruins himself. Better one handful with tranquility than two handfuls with toil and chasing after the wind. (Ecclesiastes 4:4-6)

As much as anyone who ever lived, King Solomon tried to fill his life with pleasure and excitement in an effort to find meaning in life. Whether Ecclesiastes was penned by Solomon or one of his students, the book is an account of his pursuits and the hard lessons he learned along the way. Some people read it as the complaint of a bitter old man. I don't see it that way. I think the message of that little book is the distilled wisdom of an incredibly full life and a deep desire to warn the coming generations of the temptations that can so easily distract us from the true source of contentment.

What are the things people pursue today to give their lives meaning? Look around, listen to friends, look at ads, and you'll find that there are many promises. Riches, beauty, extravagant vacations, palatial homes, sex, fame, and a host of other things are offered to us as the hope of the heart. Do they fill the gaping hole in our souls? Yes, for a brief moment, they give us exhilaration or pleasure or fleeting fame, but those things quickly fade. And when we feel empty again, how do we respond? We redouble our efforts to gain more riches, buy bigger homes, marry a sexier mate, and win even more approval from our peers—and the pace of the treadmill quickens. Solomon certainly tried all those things, but he found they couldn't fulfill their promises. His conclusion was both realistic and hopeful: don't expect those things to fill your life; follow God and enjoy every moment he gives you. That's the source of genuine contentment, and that's enough.

Today, we're bombarded with messages that we should have a certain amount of money so we can be financially secure. Certainly, the godly principles of earning, saving, and giving are clearly outlined in the Bible, but many of us are consumed with dreams of big bank accounts. Ironically, many of the people with daydreams of wealth are saddled with oppressive levels of debt. The dream and reality crash together every time they have to pay the bills. Like every manmade thing, money can't give us the ultimate contentment we long for. Solomon, the richest man in the world, observed, "Whoever loves money never has money enough; whoever loves wealth is never satisfied with his income. This too is meaningless" (Ecclesiastes 5:10).

To his followers, Jesus said, "If anyone would come after me, he must deny himself and take up his cross and follow me. For whoever wants to save his life will lose it, but whoever loses his life for me will find it. What good will it be for a man if he gains the whole world, yet forfeits his soul?" (Matthew 16:24-26) Here's a way to explain what he means. Imagine that I have an immense pair of scales. On one side, I put all the gold, silver, oil, real estate, jewelry, and everything else of value on earth. On the other side, I put a single person, maybe an obscure tribesman from the depths of the Amazon rainforest, or maybe you or me. On the balance, the weight of the one person is heavier than everything else of value on the globe. If the worth of one soul is more valuable than all the wealth in the world, why on earth would we pursue anything or anyone but the Creator who loves us so much? As Solomon wrote, it's meaningless . . . empty . . . and stupid.

I know two brothers who exemplify this choice. They were from a troubled home, and both of them longed to find significance. One brother found Christ when he was in college, and he hung around people who loved God with all their hearts. Their values rubbed off on him, and gradually, he took on their perspectives about God and life. Like all of us, he's had an up and down experience, but more times than not, he's chosen to walk with God through thick and thin. Today, he may not be perceived as the most exciting human being on the planet, but his family loves him, he has some great friends, and he has found true contentment. His brother, though, walked a very different path. Instead of turning to God, he tried to find thrills in alcohol and drugs, as much sex as he could have, and risky business deals that promised the moon. Today, he looks back at a long string of failed marriages, former friends who no longer trust him, the specter of personal bankruptcy, and a nagging sense of emptiness.

We have to be very careful which promises we believe. The ones yelled by the world can easily drown out God's quiet assurances that loving him and loving others are the pathway to genuine joy and contentment. That's our test each day: Which voice will we listen to, and which voice will we act on?

Many people live under clouds of stress and worry. They spend their energy and time trying to figure out how to escape their problems and find some semblance of joy in their lives. The one source of help many people (including many in the church) seem to forget is God. In his most famous sermon, Jesus told people, "But seek first his kingdom and his righteousness, and all these things [clothes, food, and other essentials] will be given to you as well. Therefore do not worry about tomorrow, for tomorrow will worry about itself. Each day has enough trouble of its own" (Matthew 6:33-34). Do you want to know the source of contentment? It's Jesus himself.

In his travels to tell people about Christ, Paul certainly experienced a range of responses from people. In one city, he was worshiped as a god, but the next day the same people tried to kill him! He saw incredible answers to prayer, miracles of God's grace, as well as excruciating times of suffering. The believers in Philippi sent Paul financial support and a man from the church to help him. In his thank-you letter, he shared the "secret" of contentment. He wrote, "I have learned to be content whatever the circumstances. I know what it is to be in need, and I know what it is to have plenty. I have learned the secret of being content in any and every situation, whether well fed or hungry, whether living in plenty or in want. I can do everything through him who gives me strength" (Philippians 4:11-13).

Many of us don't feel that we can be truly satisfied with God and with life unless . . . We may fill in the blank differently, but we fill it in with whatever we're convinced will give us joy or love or pleasure or excitement. The real secret, Paul says, is to stop looking at what we have or don't have, and stop comparing our lot in life with our friends or the models in ads. Instead, we drink deeply of God's love, trusting that he is using every moment and every circumstance — whether painful or pleasant — to mold our lives and give us a platform to touch others with his love. When we scrape away all the false promises and fluff, knowing and honoring Jesus is all that really matters.

A reporter once asked John D. Rockefeller, the founder of Standard Oil Company and the wealthiest man in the world, "Mr. Rockefeller, what will it take for you to be happy?"

He replied, "Just a little bit more. Just a little bit more."

I can almost hear Solomon sigh. Yes, if we try to fill the hole in our hearts with money or fame or sex or anything else, we'll always need "just a little bit more." God has made us so that only he can fill our hearts. St. Augustine once prayed, "You have made us for yourself, O Lord, and our hearts are restless until they rest in you." Listen to your heart. Is it restless or is it content? Bathe your heart with God's love, mercy, and purpose, and experience deeper, richer contentment than you ever thought possible.

How would you define or describe contentment?

What are some things your friends try to fill their lives with? What are the promises they are believing? What are the results?

In what areas of your life are you seeking contentment in things that are temporary? What are some false promises that threaten to (or actually) keep you from being truly content? What specific steps of change do you need to take?

Jesus, I want my heart to be filled with your love and purpose for my life so that...

Elijah
THE LONELINESS TEST

And the word of the Lord came to him: "What are you doing here, Elijah?" He replied, "I have been very zealous for the Lord God Almighty. The Israelites have rejected your covenant, broken down your altars, and put your prophets to death with the sword. I am the only one left, and now they are trying to kill me too." (1 Kings 19:9-10)

Counselors tell us that one of the most consuming fears in the hearts of people is the fear of being alone. We do almost anything to keep from feeling abandoned, and when those emotions sweep over us, they can devastate us. I vividly recall when two of my sons, Dillon and Hunter, were younger and Dakota wasn't even born yet. Dillon, who is a year older than Hunter, went off to kindergarten without his brother. It was a great day for Dillon, who was feeling big and cool with his Barney lunch box and Elmo backpack, but it was a very sad and lonely day for Hunter who had never been without his big brother.

As Dillon got in the car to go off to school, Hunter looked at Jenni and said, "Mom, I don't want Dillon to leave me and go to school." Jenni assured him that it would be okay and that Dillon had to go to school. Later that day, Hunter told Jenni that he was going to go outside to play with his "other brother" because his real brother left him. There was, of course, no "other brother"—it was his imaginary brother. (That was around the same time he had an imaginary dog named Pickle that drank candy milk out of his shoe. Candy milk was what Hunter called chocolate milk. He would pour it into his shoe for Pickle to drink. I promise you these issues come from Jenni's side of the family.)

Children aren't the only ones who do desperate things to keep from feeling abandoned or alone. All of us are susceptible to the despair that comes from loneliness. It can strike at almost any time. Some have lived with it for many years. They were abandoned (physically or emotionally) by their parents, and they've never felt they belonged to anyone anywhere. For most of us, though, feelings of isolation come occasionally. A trusted friend may hurt our feelings, a spouse may not pay as much attention as we'd like, a boss may overlook our work, or a child takes us for granted. In the story of Elijah, we find yet another scenario when we can experience the pangs of loneliness: in the aftermath of a glorious success.

One of the most striking and memorable dramas in the Old Testament is Elijah's confrontation with the prophets of Baal at Mount Carmel. Elijah set up a divine battle. In one corner, 450 prophets called on Baal to send fire to light the altar and sacrifice. They chanted and cut themselves for hours, but no fire came. Elijah mocked them and said, "Pray louder. Maybe he can't hear you," and then he wondered out loud, "Maybe Baal is in the bathroom. Is that the reason he's not sending fire?" Finally, their turn was over. Then, in the other corner, the challenger Elijah asked God to send fire from heaven to show the prophets, the people, and the king and queen the power of Almighty God. To show off God's power, Elijah dug a trench around the altar and drenched the wood and the animal, and filled the trenches with water. Then he prayed, "O Lord, God of Abraham, Isaac and Israel, let it be known today that you are God in Israel and that I am your servant and have done all these things at your command. Answer me, O Lord, answer me, so these people will know that you, O Lord, are God, and that you are turning their hearts back again" (1 Kings 18:36-37).

Suddenly, fire from heaven torched the sacrifice and the altar, and it dried up all the water in the trench. The people fell down and worshipped God, and then they jumped up and captured all the prophets and led them to their execution.

If there was ever a reason for any believer to be on a spiritual high, this was it. Has there ever been a more dramatic answer to prayer than this? To confirm God's power to the people, Elijah asked God to break the drought that had plagued the land for many years, and God sent a huge storm.

Hundreds of enemy prophets? No problem. Suffocating drought? Fixed in a flash. But then, Queen Jezebel sent word to Elijah that she wanted to kill him. You'd think that the past few days of glorious victories would have steeled the prophet's soul and he'd trust God to protect him against a single person's threat, but Elijah was terrified of Jezebel and ran for his life!

Elijah wasn't only afraid, he was on the edge of being suicidal. He prayed, "I've had enough, God. Let me die right now." God didn't correct his faulty thinking, and he didn't lecture the doubting prophet. First, he met his physical needs. God sent an angel with bread and water to nourish him, and Elijah enjoyed a nice, long sleep. Sometimes, sleep is an escape from our troubles, but at other times, it's a necessary ingredient to refresh us. Exhaustion and burnout are often contributing factors in depression. Many times, some rest and good food help stabilize our bodies so our minds can function more effectively.

After he woke up refreshed, God fed him again and began a conversation. He asked simply, "Elijah, why are you here?" The prophet's response was an honest (but misguided) statement of his condition. Instead of being filled with faith, Elijah wallowed in self-pity: "I've served you, but the people have abandoned you (and me). All your prophets are dead, and I'm the only one left. And Jezebel wants to kill me, too!"

God's response to the prophet's plaintive cry wasn't a theological treatise. Instead, he told Elijah to stand on the mountain in front of God. A powerful wind blew so hard that the mountain began to break up. Then an earthquake shook the ground, and after that, a fierce fire ravaged the mountainside. When everything became quiet, Elijah stood at the entrance of the cave. God asked him the same question, "Elijah, why are you here?"

The prophet hadn't learned much from God's message through nature on the mountain. He gave the same answer as before. This time, God gave him a different answer. In effect, he told him that he wasn't through with him yet. Elijah was wrong about being alone; there were still 7,000 prophets in Israel who were faithful to God. He instructed Elijah to anoint a new king over Aram and Israel, and he promised military might to protect him. To encourage him, God sent a partner, another prophet named Elisha, to join the reenergized Elijah.

One of the most important principles of facing the loneliness test is this: When we feel lonely, we need to carve out time to be alone with God. We may first need to address the physical issues of rest and nourishment so we can think clearly, but after a day or two, we need a fresh encounter with the living God.

Meeting with God isn't a time for platitudes and saying what we know we should say. We need to pour out our hearts to him, being completely honest about our hopes and fears, our dreams and dreads. When we read the psalms, we find abject honesty. The writers express the highest praise to God, but they also speak openly about their deep disappointments, their confusion, and their resentment that God didn't come through like they hoped he would. The psalms are written for our instruction. God isn't shocked when we tell him we're angry or that we think he's let us down. He's heard it all before, and he'll hear it all again. Our honesty is an open door for his Spirit to move into our hearts, remind us of truth from his word, correct our wayward thinking, and refresh our hearts.

A walk outside may not be as dramatic as the wind, earthquake, and fire Elijah witnessed on the mountain, but some extended time at a park or riding a bike can clear our heads and help us see God's grandeur in nature again. Sometimes, just getting outside works wonders on our perspective.

Last Christmas I was thinking about the recurring concept in Isaiah and the gospels about the incarnation's meaning. The name Emmanuel isn't just another label for the baby Jesus at Christmas. It means "God with us," and it communicates an essential part of his nature. He never leaves us or abandons us. The Lord of the universe—the Creator and sustainer of everything we see and can't see—is present with us all day every day, including this very moment. The first couple was created to have a relationship with God. Yes, they blew it, but God didn't give up on them. Over and over again in the Old Testament, God made his presence obvious to his people, always pointing to a day when God himself would take on human flesh to live among us. As he lived with us, Jesus experienced the full range of joys and troubles. The writer to the Hebrews says that Jesus sympathizes with our weaknesses because he experienced them, too, but without sinning. There's nothing we face that he doesn't understand.

When Jesus told his followers that he was going back to the Father, he promised to send the Holy Spirit, not only to teach and guide, but to take up residence inside each one of us! It doesn't get any more relational than that. But the presence of the Spirit in us now is only a down payment, a deposit, a foreshadowing of the day when we'll be with Jesus face to face. On that day, our present bodies will be transformed into new ones like his, with new eyes and ears to take in all the senses of being in relationship with the Almighty God forever.

Before that day, though, we're completely and very human. Like the psalmists, we have swings of experience from elation to discouragement, and we all face times of loneliness. These may come when someone hurts our feelings, when we find ourselves in new relationships and we feel insecure, or when we're physically and emotionally exhausted after a glorious spiritual victory. They can happen anytime to any of us. When we feel utterly alone and full of self-pity, we need physical refreshment and spiritual encouragement. Don't neglect either one. After you've had a good meal or two and a good long sleep, encounter the living God who is with you always, to the end of the age and to the extremes of human experience. Bask in his presence and his love, and realize that you aren't alone after all.

One of the most powerful and beautiful answers to loneliness in my life is that God occasionally sends someone to speak words of encouragement to me. Almost always, they come at a time when I really need a word from God, but they seem to come from out of the blue. Not long ago, a lady came up to me after church and said some very kind things to me. She had no idea I'd been struggling with some problems. Her message and her demeanor touched my heart and warmed my soul. Years ago, I might have dismissed this conversation as just a kind, human touch because I would have been so busy shaking hands, but recently, God has given me more sensitivity to him and to the people he sends to speak into my loneliness. She said, "Pastor Scott, God wants you to know that he's proud of you and that you are right where you are supposed to be, doing what he wants you to do. He is with you."

I love it when God "winks" at me and reminds me that he's there. When I realize I'm not alone, I can encourage others with the same transforming truth.

When do you tend to feel lonely? How do you think and act during those times?

When we face loneliness, why is it essential to address the physical component as well as the spiritual one?

As you look back over your life, in what ways has God revealed to you that he is present with you in times of loneliness?

Jesus, when I feel lonely, I need to...

Naaman
THE HUMILITY TEST

Naaman's servants went to him and said, "My father, if the prophet had told you to do some great thing, would you not have done it? How much more, then, when he tells you, 'Wash and be cleansed'!" (2 Kings 5:13)

When we read the Bible, we need to have a little bit of creativity to imagine what was going on in each scene. Naaman was the top general in the Syrian army. When I think of him, I remember the look in George C. Scott's eyes when he played the lead role in the movie *Patton*. Man, that guy was tough as nails! I don't think Naaman was any different. In fact, since his culture endorsed torture and murder, he may have made Patton look like a sweet guy. But the general had an embarrassing health problem: he had leprosy.

A patrol from Naaman's army of Arameans went on a raid and captured a girl from Israel, and the writer tells us, "She served Naaman's wife." The girl must have been treated reasonably well, because she offered some advice for Naaman's skin disease. She suggested that he travel to see the prophet Elisha and ask him to heal the disease. The general got permission from the king, and he left with a formal letter from the king and a huge amount of money to pay for his healing.

Of course, his first stop was at the palace of Israel's king. When he read the letter, the king felt completely helpless and exposed. He thought he had to cure the general—and if he failed, he was sure he would be tortured to death. Elisha heard the news about the general's visit and the king's despair, and he sent a message to the king: "No problem. Send him to me."

A day or two later, Naaman and his entourage of soldiers, horses, and chariots pulled up in front of Elisha's house. I can imagine the general's anticipation. He knew how to exercise authority, and he was sure Elisha would come out, wave his hands, and poof, the leprosy would vanish.

It didn't happen quite that way. Elisha didn't even bother to come to the door. He sent a servant with his instructions to the general: "Go, wash yourself seven times in the Jordan, and your flesh will be restored and you will be cleansed" (2 Kings 5:10).

General Naaman wasn't amused. He felt deeply offended and humiliated, and he was furious! The guy didn't even bother to speak to the powerful general who had come so far and humbled himself to ask for help, and he told him to wash in some backwash stream. He could at least have told him to bathe in one of the great rivers of Syria!

Naaman's servants offered him some advice (probably at the risk of their lives), and they convinced him to do what Elisha had commanded. The great commander went to the little river and walked in. Once, twice, three times. Did he think, "What the heck am I doing? This makes no sense at all!" Whatever he thought, he continued until the seventh time, and his leprosy vanished completely. The general and his soldiers concluded, "Now I know that there is no God in all the world except in Israel."

How many times does God ask us to do things that we might consider "beneath" us? In our families, at work, and at church, many of us expand our influence, and with it, our authority. We've proven to be effective, and we expect some perks to go along with the hours and sweat we expend for others. But from time to time, God gives us an instruction that turns our self-perception upside down. He asks us to do something that seems, to be painfully honest, far beneath our stature as leaders. That moment is a test for us just like it was for Naaman. Like the general's experience, the test of humility may focus on our willingness to accept God's grace in a way that is uncomfortable to us. More often, it involves stooping to patiently serve others.

Moms like my wife Jenni know the test of humility more than most of us. Many mothers have had (or certainly could have had) positions of prestige in the corporate world, but they have chosen a lower position or no position at all in order to devote themselves to their kids. Jenni doesn't resent being a mom; she's dedicated to be the very best mother she can be. We've had many conversations when she wondered if she was doing all she could do to raise our boys to have godly character and biblical values. Jenni could have been anything she wanted to be, but she chose to devote herself to God and our kids.

People who work with us in our offices and factories are expected to perform at a high level, but they aren't machines. They have real hopes and hurts. Sometimes, they need us to take time to care, to listen, and to move into their lives in a new way to offer support and find resources. Is that our job? No, it's not written in our company's job description, but it's our role as servants of Christ. And in churches, it's easy for people to put leaders up on a pedestal, but God has a way of knocking us off. No matter how powerful we may become, God's directive is to be humble, to stoop, and to serve over and over again (Naaman bathed seven times)—without demanding anything in return. That's a true mark of humility, and it's a test we face each day.

Paul wrote the Philippians, "Do nothing out of selfish ambition or vain conceit, but in humility consider others better than yourselves. Each of you should look not only to your own interests, but also to the interests of others. Your attitude should be the same as that of Christ

Jesus" (Philippians 2:3-5). Like Naaman, we may chafe when God asks us to do something we consider beneath us, but that's exactly what Christ did. He's the ultimate example of humility. He came, he gave, he served, and he bled and died. Who am I to think that I deserve a higher role, a more acclaimed position, or an easier life than his?

It's human nature to want to be perceived as important and powerful. And when we achieve that position, we want to cling to it and protect it at all costs. However, the joy of a promotion only lasts a short while. Pretty soon, we're eyeing the next rung up the ladder. One of the biggest benchmarks of Christian maturity is our willingness to accept God's assignments to move down the ladder instead of always clamoring up. I know the president of a bank who has made it a practice to spend time each week working with people in the mailroom and the janitors. He doesn't announce this work to the rest of the company, and he doesn't stand aloof in the mailroom and give them advice. He rolls up his sleeves and pitches in. "It's the least I can do," he told me. "They are just as much a part of our team as the people who sell a million dollars of our services."

I believe God offers us opportunities each day to pass or fail the humility test. Most of them aren't as dramatic as Naaman washing in the Jordan. Instead, they involve moments to value others more than ourselves, to listen to them instead of talking about our own agendas, to notice their needs instead of focusing only on ours, and taking steps to serve people who may be lower on the organizational chart in our homes, at work, and in our churches.

We admire powerful and beautiful people, but power, prestige, and beauty aren't the measures of a believer. It's a humble heart coupled with a servant's actions, expecting nothing in return. Naaman had to wrestle with the test of humility and determine that obeying God wasn't beneath him. You and I are tested in the same way. Naaman's servants had the courage to speak the truth to him and give him good advice. I hope you and I have friends like that. We need them, and we need to listen to them.

Think of powerful and beautiful people you know. What are some things they might consider beneath them?

What do you think was going on in Naaman's mind when his servants suggested that he follow Elisha's directions and wash in the Jordan?

What are some ways you face the test of humility today? What have you considered beneath you that God's Spirit is now saying you need to do to obey God?

Jesus, you are the epitome of humility. I want to be more like you so that...

Shadrach, Meshach, and Abednego
THE LOYALTY TEST

Shadrach, Meshach and Abednego replied to the king, "O Nebuchadnezzar, we do not need to defend ourselves before you in this matter. If we are thrown into the blazing furnace, the God we serve is able to save us from it, and he will rescue us from your hand, O king. But even if he does not, we want you to know, O king, that we will not serve your gods or worship the image of gold you have set up." (Daniel 3:16-18)

Daniel and his three friends were foreigners in the most powerful nation on earth. King Nebuchadnezzar had conquered most of the known world, and to honor himself, he erected a 90-foot gold statue on the plain of Dura to remind everybody of his power. He also instructed the people of his kingdom to bow down before the statue whenever they heard his musicians play. Anyone who refused would be thrown into a furnace to be burned. There were three men, though, who refused to bow: Shadrach, Meshach, and Abednego. When the king found out, he was furious. They, like Daniel, had been chosen from all the Israelite young men to be pampered by the king's men so they could serve him. Now, Nebuchadnezzar saw, they repaid this privilege with rebellion.

The king was furious, and he gave them one last chance to worship the statue. Still, they refused. This time, they told him to his face that their God is certainly able to rescue them, but even if he doesn't, they're committed to remain faithful to him. In a fit of rage, the king ordered the furnace to be heated seven times hotter. He told his strongest soldiers to tie up the three men and throw them into the fire. When the soldiers carrying the men approached the opening of the furnace, the fire was so hot they burned up! Nothing and no one, the king was sure, could survive in those flames. But a few seconds later, he saw figures moving in the furnace. In fact, there were four men there! He said, "Look! I see four men walking around in the fire, unbound and unharmed, and the fourth looks like a son of the gods."

Nebuchadnezzar called to the men to come out of the fire, but only three emerged. All the members of the court crowded around them, and they saw that the flames hadn't singed a single hair on their heads. The king recognized the significance of their faith, but even more, the power of their God. Instead of forcing them to renounce their faith in God, the king now honored the God of these three remarkable men. Never one to be accused of having a soft side, Nebuchadnezzar announced, "Praise be to the God of Shadrach, Meshach and Abednego, who has sent his angel and rescued his servants! They trusted in him and defied the king's command and were willing to give up their lives rather than serve or worship any god except their own God. Therefore I decree that the people of any nation or language who say anything against the God of Shadrach, Meshach and Abednego be cut into pieces and their houses be turned into piles of rubble, for no other god can save in this way."

When we read the Old Testament, it's easy to think, "Oh, that was so long ago. I'm not sure it has any relevance to my world today." Yes, it certainly was a different time and a different culture, but the principles are just as relevant today as they were over 2,500 years ago. Most of the time, Daniel and his friends enjoyed a life of ease in a foreign land. Paul tells us that we are citizens of heaven. While we walk in this life, we are foreigners here, enjoying many of the same pampered benefits of wealth and comfort Daniel and his friends enjoyed. The temptation for them was to think that they could just sit back and sink into their new culture, forgetting their commitment to God, or fudging their commitment whenever faith in him became inconvenient. And a 90-foot statue? Our culture has erected an enormous statue of beauty, wealth, possessions, and prestige that everyone is encouraged to worship.

The three Jewish friends in Nebuchadnezzar's kingdom could have found a dozen excuses to bow to the statue: It would save their lives, they could relate more easily to others in the kingdom, and it would certainly make life easier for them. But they chose God over comfort, faith over despair, and obedience to God over bailing out to the pressures of the king and his soldiers.

The measure of a person's loyalty is found in his willingness to pay a price for the one he serves. For the three friends, the cost stared them in the face: death in the furnace. To us, the cost usually is subtle: inconvenience, a word of sarcasm from our friends who don't understand, or being passed over because we're "too weird" or "too religious."

One of the biggest tests of our lives is submission: will we remain loyal to God when things don't go smoothly and when we don't get what we think we deserve? Dr. Tim Keller is the pastor of Redeemer Presbyterian Church in Manhattan. He warned, "Don't confuse your agenda for God with your faith in God." When we go to God with a set of expectations about how he should treat us, that's not faith; it's a demand. The three friends exhibited true faith, knowing that God could rescue them, but certain of his goodness and faithfulness even if he didn't. Their submission and loyalty weren't colored by any expectations of how God "should" work in their lives. The list of the faithful people in Hebrews 11 begins with people who saw God do miraculous things in their lives, but true faith doesn't guarantee God's miracles. We read about people who were tortured, ridiculed, beaten, put in chains and thrown into prison. Some were stoned to death, some killed by swords, and one was sawn in two. These faithful men and women wandered in deserts and endured harsh conditions of extreme poverty—because they stayed true to God in spite of the pressures of their culture. If submission is measured by the cost of loyalty, these people demonstrated their faith boldly and clearly!

Several years ago, a beautiful young woman named Amy Pomykal faced the submission test. Her life was going really well. She was a flight attendant, and she had recently gotten married. One day, however, Amy had a seizure and passed out. The doctor conducted tests and gave her the dreaded news: a brain tumor. She came over to our house often to talk with Jenni and me. I'll never forget her faith in that difficult hour of her life. With a heart full of trust in God no matter what happened, she told us, "I know God can heal me, but even if he doesn't, I'll use every breath I have until I die to worship him, serve him, and tell everyone who will listen about his love and greatness."

I was so moved by her faith that I asked her to share her story in church. As a church family, we prayed for God to heal Amy, but we trusted that he would be honored by her life or her death. Three years later, after rounds of chemotherapy, the doctors pronounced that she was cancer-free. We all rejoiced in her healing, but her example helped all of us trust God a little more with our own difficulties, no matter how he answered.

Difficult times—like furnaces, tumors, financial setbacks, and the shattering of relationships—are tests of our submission to God. Dr. J. I. Packer observed, "Sooner or later, God's guidance, which brings us out of darkness into light, will also bring us out of light into darkness. It's part of the way of the cross."[10] The way of the cross always involves tests of submission.

---

10 Packer, *Knowing God*, p. 219.

What are some tests of submission you've faced?

What are some ways we can tell if and when we've confused *our agenda for* God with *our faith in* God? Have you been confused in this way? If you have, explain your answer.

Describe what it means to you to be completely loyal to God no matter what happens.

Father, you are worthy of my complete submission and loyalty. Today, I want to be...

Daniel
THE IDENTITY TEST

So the administrators and the satraps went as a group to the king and said: "O King Darius, live forever! The royal administrators, prefects, satraps, advisers and governors have all agreed that the king should issue an edict and enforce the decree that anyone who prays to any god or man during the next thirty days, except to you, O king, shall be thrown into the lions' den." Now when Daniel learned that the decree had been published, he went home to his upstairs room where the windows opened toward Jerusalem. Three times a day he got down on his knees and prayed, giving thanks to his God, just as he had done before. (Daniel 6:6-7, 10)

Talk about pressure! Daniel had been captured in his native land and hauled away to Babylon. There, he wasn't made a normal slave. Instead, Nebuchadnezzar ordered his top general to select a few Hebrew young men to serve the throne. Daniel and the other chosen Israelites were given the finest foods to help them look strong and healthy, and their names were changed to fit their new culture. Day and night, they received instruction to brainwash them. Their captors wanted the men to forget their old ways and their old God and embrace Babylon as their adopted land.

Through cunning and violence, Darius the Persian became king of the empire. He recognized the need for good administration of the kingdom, and he appointed 120 governors over the land, to be ruled by three supervisors, including Daniel. The young Hebrew proved to be especially gifted in administration, so Darius planned to put him in charge of the entire kingdom. Powerful people are often jealous. It's true in our day, and it was true in Persia. The supervisors and governors wanted to find a way to bring Daniel down. They couldn't attack his work—it was excellent. They couldn't accuse him of graft and corruption—his character was impeccable. The only angle they could find was that Daniel had remained true to God instead of bowing to Babylonian or Persian gods.

The leaders wrote a new law to forbid praying to anyone but King Darius for 30 days. Anyone who transgressed this law would be torn to bits and devoured by lions. They knew Daniel prayed regularly, so they were sure where the next meal for the lions would come from.

Like all of us—at pivotal moments in our lives but also in everyday decisions—Daniel was caught between loyalty to God and pressure to bend to the culture. He chose God. He decided to continue to pray, but not in a closet. Three times a day, he opened his window and prayed in full view of anyone who was watching. As he fully expected, his rivals reported his actions to the king, and he was thrown to the lions.

The point of the lesson in this chapter isn't that God miraculously closed the mouths of the lions so that Daniel walked away without a scratch. He didn't know God would do that for him. He chose to live for God—no matter what the cost. His identity, his essence, his very being was to be God's man, whether he was in Israel or in Persia. It didn't matter to him.

Paul wrote the Romans, "Do not conform any longer to the pattern of this world, but be transformed by the renewing of your mind. Then you will be able to test and approve what God's will is—his good, pleasing and perfect will" (Romans 12:2). For Daniel, the pattern of the world was a line in the sand over the issue of loyalty. He was willing to become one of the king's servants, eating the best foods and receiving the finest teaching on the planet, because these didn't compromise his loyalty to God. However, when he faced the law requiring him to pray to a man instead of God, he refused. His conscience was a measure of God's will, and he made a choice that would probably cost him his life. Nothing could cause him to choose anyone or anything over God.

Loyalty is a function of identity. What is our sense of identity? When someone asks, "Who are you?", what comes to mind? Many of us say where we're from, we tell our occupation, or we may talk about our family heritage. When John described his identity, he said he was "the one Jesus loved." Does that mean he was the only one Jesus loved? Of course not, but he was so overwhelmed with the kindness and affection of Christ that it became the source of John's identity. Peter calls us "aliens and strangers" as we walk around on earth, and Paul wrote, "Our citizenship is in heaven." In a sense, we don't belong here. He also wrote the Corinthians that we've "been bought with a price" so we're "not our own." Our possessions and the approval of our friends aren't the ultimate sources of our identity. And our jobs are important, but only as they give us a platform to reflect God's character and the abilities he's given us. A multitude of forces and voices try to pressure us to give in, to choose the easy way or the exciting way over God's way. When our identity is squarely rooted in God, we'll choose loyalty to him over anything else.

We need to be careful, though, that we don't go haywire with this. Remember that the line in the sand with Daniel was at the public display of loyalty. He was willing to put up with some other things, and even to serve faithfully in the king's administration. For us, too, we can use the opportunities the world gives us, and we can serve enthusiastically and effectively in our jobs and in civic groups, but somewhere, there has to be a line that defines who we are, what we value, and who we serve.

For 50 years, Bishop Clay Evans served as the founding pastor of the Fellowship Missionary Baptist Church in Chicago. Bishop Evans was active in the Civil Rights Movement, and in the height of racial tension in the nation, he asked Dr. Martin Luther King to speak at this church. At the time, the church was building a new, large auditorium, and of course, every permit and inspection had to pass through city officials. Mayor Richard Daley heard about the invitation. He called Bishop Evans and expressed his concern about the possibility of riots in the city in protest to Dr. King, and he asked Evans to withdraw the invitation. He declined. Daley then upped the ante: "If you have Dr. King speak at your church, the next day every construction crane, every piece of scaffolding, every concrete truck, and every worker will vanish from your building site."

Bishop Evans calmly replied, "Mayor Daley, Jesus Christ is Lord of this church, and the gates of hell will not prevail against it. Sir, you can make any choice you want to make, but ultimately, you will not prevail."

Dr. King came to Chicago and spoke at Bishop Evans' church. The very next day, every piece of construction equipment and machinery was taken from the site. All that was left was a naked steel structure, and it stood as a silent sentinel for seven years. Week after week, Bishop Evans and his people walked around in the bare concrete among the steel braces and prayed, "Lord, do what you will here. This is your place. We're not going to bow to the man, God. We're going to keep following you."

When the permits were renewed and construction resumed, the people rejoiced. They were thrilled when the building finally opened, but that's not the real story. Those seven years when the unfinished building was only a slab and beams were a testimony to a man of God who refused to compromise. Bishop Evans' actions and faith provided an example of faithfulness to God in the face of government pressure, and he wouldn't back down a single inch. The integrity he demonstrated during that time gave him a strong, vibrant identity, and the entire city sat up and noticed.

The identity test for us often comes in unexpected moments: when we choose which channels to watch or web sites to view, when we can sneak some money from an account without anyone noticing or we can choose to be honest, when someone has some juicy gossip about a friend and we choose to listen or not, and a thousand other decisions every day. They may seem insignificant, but they reflect *who* we believe we are—and more important, *whose* we believe we are.

The world is watching to see if we'll tell the truth and do the honorable thing, or whether we'll blame someone else, be selfish, choose comfort over compassion, pick convenience over justice, or lie to keep from accepting responsibility. You might say, "Aren't these tests of honesty and integrity?" Yes, but at a deeper level, they are tests of our sense of who we are—our identity. As Jesus explained, if we try to save our life, we'll lose it, but if we lose our lives for his sake, we'll find more peace, joy, and fulfillment than we ever imagined. It's all about who we believe we are.

What do most people use to define or describe their sense of identity?

What are some choices you've faced in the past week that are determined by how you see yourself? How did you do?

How does it (or might it) affect your choices if you see yourself as "the person Jesus loves," an "alien and stranger" on earth, with your "citizenship in heaven"?

Lord, I'm yours today, and that means...

Nehemiah
THE PERSEVERANCE
TEST

> Therefore I stationed some of the people behind the lowest points of the wall at the exposed places, posting them by families, with their swords, spears and bows. After I looked things over, I stood up and said to the nobles, the officials and the rest of the people, "Don't be afraid of them. Remember the Lord, who is great and awesome, and fight for your brothers, your sons and your daughters, your wives and your homes." (Nehemiah 4:13-14)

The Bible includes some wonderful stories about individual bravery, but the account of Nehemiah leading the people of Jerusalem to rebuild the walls is one of the most stirring narratives of a leader inspiring others to act courageously. In the face of incredible odds, he persevered in trusting God to give him the king's favor, resources, and wisdom to turn discouraged people into lions of faith.

Nehemiah was a cupbearer to the Persian King Artaxerxes. Word came to him that his people in Judah were in trouble and "full of shame." The protective walls of Jerusalem had been broken down, and its gates had been burned. When Nehemiah heard this report, his heart broke, and he cried for several days. He reminded God of his covenant with the Jewish nation, and he confessed his people's sins against God. The king noticed that Nehemiah looked sad, and he asked, "Why does your face look so sad when you are not ill? This can be nothing but sadness of heart" (Nehemiah 2:2). Nehemiah told him about the condition of Jerusalem, and the king asked, "What do you want?"

His first response wasn't to make a long list of supplies required to rebuild the city walls. Instead, Nehemiah instantly prayed, and only then did he ask for the king's favor and for the supplies he needed. The king must have been impressed with Nehemiah's integrity and leadership skills because he gave him everything required to get the job done—everything except laborers.

When Nehemiah came to Jerusalem, he found the reports were true: the city walls were only heaps of rocks. But as he enlisted the people to help him rebuild, he may not have anticipated all the obstacles he faced. Sanballat, Nehemiah's self-appointed adversary, wondered aloud, " 'What are those feeble Jews doing? Will they restore their wall? Will they offer sacrifices? Will they finish in a day? Can they bring the stones back to life from those heaps of rubble—burned as they are?' Tobiah the Ammonite, who was at his side, said, 'What they are building—if even a fox climbed up on it, he would break down their wall of stones!' " (Nehemiah 4:2-3) The men working on the walls were discouraged, tired, and ready to give up. More enemies threatened to kill Nehemiah and the workers, and Jews who lived nearby complained ten times that the enemies would attack them too, even if they didn't help rebuild the wall!

Nehemiah could have looked at all the obstacles and listened to all the complaints and given up, but he didn't. Instead, he recast the vision and developed a strategic plan. He wrote, "Therefore I stationed some of the people behind the lowest points of the wall at the exposed places, posting them by families, with their swords, spears and bows. After I looked things over, I stood up and said to the nobles, the officials and the rest of the people, 'Don't be afraid of them. Remember the Lord, who is great and awesome, and fight for your brothers, your sons and your daughters, your wives and your homes' " (Nehemiah 4:13-14). I wish I could have been there to hear that message!

Nehemiah's courage and clear plan inspired his workers and discouraged his enemies, but he didn't let down his guard. From that day on, he instructed half of his people to carry weapons while the other half worked on the walls. To stay ready for battle, they kept their weapons ready—even when they went to the bathroom. In only 52 days and in spite of fierce opposition and discouragement, Nehemiah's workers rebuilt the wall. It's an incredible story of a leader's determination and perseverance.

I'm afraid that there's a strain of teaching in the church today that's very misleading and confusing. Sometimes, I hear someone say, "We just need to sit back and watch God work." Watching God at work is a very good thing, but we don't have to sit back to see it. And sometimes I hear people say, "If it takes any effort on our part, we're not really trusting God. It should be all him and nothing of us." Wow, Nehemiah would be shocked to hear statements like that! Walking with God isn't stepping back and watching God do everything for us. Most often, it's trusting God to lead us, equip us, and empower us to be partners with him in touching people's lives. Being passive for God may sound very spiritual, but it's not the way God normally works. Spirit-prompted activity is the normal Christian life—full of boldness, courage, and tenacity. Of course, we don't want to trust only in ourselves, but we need to remember that God most often uses people like us in his work. It's our task (and our privilege) to listen carefully to him, to obey his leading, and take bold steps to change lives. That's what Nehemiah modeled for us, and that's how God works in churches today. Passivity doesn't stand a chance against real opposition from God's enemies.

A few years ago, I was asked to go to Israel to speak at a youth convention for Messianic Jewish students. When I spoke, I sensed God prompting me to tell them that they would be a generation who would follow the example of John the Baptist to announce the coming of the Messiah to their nation—and like John, they could expect to be misunderstood and persecuted for their bold faith. It was their duty, I assured them, to persevere to fulfill God's assignment for them.

During those days at the youth convention, we experienced intense spiritual struggles. Leaders got sick and were healed, people wrestled with the truth of God's word, and I sensed opposition to my messages. But we also experienced God's powerful anointing. In those days, God touched students' hearts in amazing ways. Seven of the students trusted in Yeshua (Jesus) as their Messiah.

One day, a reporter from the leading national newspaper came to see what was going on at the convention. For several days, she listened intently and took some pictures. She seemed really nice, and we enjoyed hosting her. We trusted God to work in her life just like he was working in the students' lives. When the convention ended, we said goodbye to her and wished her well. A short time later, someone brought me a newspaper with a full-page article about our meetings. I asked our translator to read the Hebrew caption under my picture. In a sheepish voice, she reluctantly read: "Scott Wilson, the chubby American, tells Israeli students, 'Give me the lights, give me the music, and I'll tell you of the real religion of who God is.'" The article falsely reported that we locked kids in their room and wouldn't let them out until they accepted Yeshua as the Messiah. It also claimed that we enticed them with food, American music, and other treats if they'd believe our message.

Not surprisingly, the article created a national uproar against the ministry that invited us to speak. The leaders of the sponsoring organization fought the report in the judicial system, some of the students' phones were bugged, and others were beaten up. Still, many people came each week to the local congregation to see what all the fuss was about, and they heard the message about the Messiah who loves them enough to die for them. This group of students and their leaders suffered obstacles, accusations, and attacks like Nehemiah and his workers endured, and like them, these modern believers stayed strong in the face of opposition. In the end, the congregation grew, the students' faith blossomed, and they won their lawsuit against the company that published the libelous article. One of these students eventually became the youth pastor. You can imagine the stories he can tell about God's faithfulness when his people are attacked!

When we experience obstacles and setbacks today, do we think, "Man, that's really bad luck," or do we see every moment through the lens of God's truth? We're in a spiritual battle—for our own souls, our families, and for our communities. We shouldn't be surprised when we step out for God and obstacles appear out of nowhere and enemies attack us. Nehemiah didn't let anything or anyone deter him from accomplishing the task God had given him, but on the other hand, he didn't just bull his way through and bruise people along the way. No, he was a compassionate and determined leader of men and women. He depended on God, but he wasn't passive in the least. He trusted God to provide direction and resources, and he inspired those around him with a clear vision, a strategic plan, and a model of bold perseverance.

How do most people respond to obstacles and opposition? How do you normally respond?

Nehemiah experienced his people's discouragement, betrayal by friends, and threats by enemies. Which of these would have been most difficult for you to endure? Explain your answer.

Do you need to persevere through a difficulty in your life right now? What are some principles from Nehemiah's life that give you encouragement and direction?

Father, I want to stay strong during this tough time. Help me to...

Job
THE CONFUSION TEST

Though he slay me, yet will I hope in him;

I will surely defend my ways to his face.

Indeed, this will turn out for my deliverance,

for no godless man would dare come before him! (Job 13:15-16)

The story of Job is the grad school of testing. Throughout the history of the faith, people have looked to him as an example of faith under fire. All of the calamities he endured seemed to come out of the blue, and no one (no human, that is) had any answers to his piercing questions. One of the most difficult tests we face is confusion. When we can identify the source of our struggles, we feel more confident that we can find a way out or through them, but when we don't have a clue how we got into a predicament, it's easy to give up in despair. Throughout Job's entire ordeal, even when he was misunderstood and maligned by his wife and his friends, he continued to pursue God. That's one of the hardest lessons we will ever learn.

The "wisdom literature" in the Bible is an interesting blend of books. Proverbs gives us a clear sense of cause and effect in the universe. Sinful choices reap negative consequences, and wise decisions lead to kingdom prosperity and relationships based on trust. The law of the harvest is the hallmark of Proverbs. But not so fast. In Ecclesiastes, we learn that things aren't so clear and simple. The good suffer and die just like evil people, and the seasons come and go in endless cycles without regard to anyone's choices. The message of this book is that we need to go deeper into the heart of God to find wisdom. Job, however, turns the law of the harvest upside down and inside out! A good and righteous man experiences the most horrible problems we can imagine, and there's no visible cause he can point to. He is, for most of the book, confused . . . very confused.

As the readers, we know some things Job never discovers. The backdrop of the story is a cosmic conversation between Satan and God. Satan accuses Job of trusting God only because God blesses him so much, so God gives him permission to test Job with difficulties. Soon, messengers run to tell Job the horrible news. The first one reports that thieves stole all the oxen and donkeys and killed every servant except the one who brought the report. While he was telling this news, another ran in to tell Job that in a different field, a lightning storm killed all of his sheep and every servant except the one who told him this horrific news. Before he finished, a third ran in and told Job that the Babylonians swept in to steal all of his camels and killed (you guessed it) all the servants except the lone messenger. The fourth report was, though, the most difficult to hear. Another man ran in and told Job that a great wind caused the house to collapse, and it killed all of his sons and daughters. I've heard a cascade of bad news before, but nothing so tragic and overwhelming as this. Job's response showed his steadfast faith in God's goodness and sovereignty. He said,

"Naked I came from my mother's womb,
    and naked I will depart.
The Lord gave and the Lord has taken away;
    may the name of the Lord be praised" (Job 1:21).

God was impressed with Job's faith, but Satan insisted on more tests. He told God that Job would surely deny his faith if he allowed Satan to cause bodily harm to Job. God agreed to the test, and Satan caused Job to experience painful boils from the sole of his feet to the top of his head. Now, these weren't pimples. Boils are deep infections that are painful and ugly. When Job's wife saw her husband scraping his infected skin with a piece of pottery, she barked, "Just curse God and die!"

Again, Job refused to give up on God's goodness. He replied to his angry wife, "You are talking like a foolish woman. Shall we accept good from God, and not trouble?" (Job 2:10)

Much of the rest of the book consists of conversations between Job and his friends. They believed that God always operates in the cause-effect realm of the Proverbs, so their conclusion was that Job's problems surely were a direct result of some horrible sin he had committed. That, they were convinced, was the only plausible reason for his problems. Over and over again, they insisted that he "come clean" and admit he had sinned, but at every point, Job protested that he was innocent. Throughout the painful accusations of his friends, Job kept asking for a meeting with God so he could ask what in the world was going on. No matter how many false accusations he endured and how confused he was, Job never gave up on God. He said, "Though he slay me, yet will I hope in him." That's faith that transcends confusion.

Finally, God granted the interview. When "God showed up," he didn't enter a dialogue that Job anticipated. Instead, God asked his confused follower a series of 64 penetrating questions. Basically, the questions were, "Who are you to question my actions? I'm the Creator of the universe. How can you think you know more about life than I do?"

After God finished asking all those questions, Job responded with humility. He said, "Surely I spoke of things I did not understand, things too wonderful for me to know" (Job 42:3). It's interesting to note that God never answered Job's question of "why" the tragedies happened.

He only said, in effect, "I'm God and you're not. Sometimes, you just have to trust me." In times of confusion, we don't know why we're going through struggles, and the lesson of Job is that we may never know. Still, God calls us to focus on his character, his love, and his majesty. Even when we don't know what's going on, we can be sure that he does—and he is good.

Because we're human, it's easy for us to fix our hearts on God's blessings and expect him to always work in certain ways in our lives. Sooner or later, though, God's path leads us into a dead end, a box canyon, or a blind alley. In those times, we can cry out to God for answers, but he may only say to us, "On this side of heaven, you're not going to know the reasons. For now, you're just going to have to trust me." We can protest that our suffering isn't fair, and we can complain that it doesn't make any sense at all, but in those times our insistence on answers becomes a roadblock for our faith. Like Job, we need to look at the greatness of God and know there are things that are "too wonderful for us to know." In the end, God blessed Job with prosperity again, and God himself rebuked his friends for their false assumptions.

When Jenni was pregnant with our second child, we experienced the test of confusion. At a regular check up on a Friday early in her pregnancy, the doctor couldn't find the baby's heartbeat. He announced that he was scheduling a D&C for Monday to remove the baby. All weekend, we struggled with God. We told him, "Lord, we sure want this baby to live, but we're yours. Do with us what you want to." We thought about all the things that had happened since we first heard the news Jenni was pregnant, but we couldn't figure out any reason for the problem. On Monday, the doctor listened again, and this time he heard the baby's heartbeat. We were elated and deeply relieved. The weekend, though, forced us to dig deeper into the heart of God. In the crucible of that terrifying and confusing moment, we determined to trust him no matter what.

Most of us say we want to know Christ, but comparatively few are willing to pay the price to go deeper into the relationship to know him more intimately. Knowing him in the core of our souls isn't the stuff of happy talk and spiritual fluff. Tucked into a wonderful letter to thank people for supporting his ministry, Paul gives us a glimpse of what it means to go deeper with God. He wrote, "I want to know Christ and the power of his resurrection and the fellowship of sharing in his sufferings, becoming like him in his death" (Philippians 3:10). Oh, we love the part about experiencing the power of his resurrection, but knowing him also involves sharing in his sufferings and becoming like him in his death. Does our model of a walk of faith include those things? If not, our faith will remain shallow and weak. Times of suffering have a way of stripping away the fluff from our lives and driving us deeper into the heart of God. When we're struggling, we don't just go through the motions. Like never before, we need to know God and experience his power, grace, and love. Yes, we're thrilled by the miracle moments of seeing God work in incredible ways, but we'll never really know God intimately until and unless we share in his suffering and sacrifice our comfort and prestige on a cross for God's sake like he did. For me, not being able to connect the dots of cause-and-effect causes me to pursue God more than ever.

When we experience confusion, we enroll in the grad school of testing. These are some of the most difficult days of our lives, and unfortunately, there are many people in the church who are like Job's friends, only too eager to tell us that it's all our fault! Certainly, we need to be open to the Spirit's tap on our shoulders to show us our responsibility, and most often, the cause can be traced to some kind of sin or dumb mistake. From time to time, however, we'll be totally perplexed about the cause of our suffering. In those days, we need to follow Job's example. We keep asking God to show up, we never give up on him, and we learn the deepest lessons of our lives: to trust in God's goodness and greatness no matter what.

Have you ever gone through a time of confusion when you couldn't identify the cause of your struggles? How did you feel, and how did you respond at that time?

Describe the kind of faith it takes to be able to say (and really mean): "Though he slay me, yet will I hope in him."

Why do you think God's answer to Job's questions was a set of questions without really answering his specific questions? How would you have responded to God's 64 questions? How are you responding to those questions now?

Father, you are God and I'm not. I trust you because...

Mary
THE "YES" TEST

"I am the Lord's servant," Mary answered. "May it be to me as you have said." Then the angel left her. (Luke 1:38)

One of the most remarkable encounters in the Scriptures occurred when an angel appeared to a young woman and announced that she was going to be the mother of God's Messiah. Mary was engaged to marry Joseph. Her plans were set, but her heart was open to God. Her answer to Gabriel's pronouncement was a resounding "yes." In fact, I believe her heart had said "yes" to God long before Gabriel appeared to her that day. Her attitude was, "God, the answer is always 'yes.' Now, what's your question?"

It's hard to imagine the shock of that moment for Mary. Angels aren't chubby little babies depicted on Valentine's Day cards. They are awesome beings with enormous power! Throughout the Bible, when an angel appeared to someone, his first words usually were: "Don't be afraid." Why did angels almost universally begin this way? Because the sight of them terrified people!

Gabriel assured Mary of God's favor, and he explained that she would have this special child even though she wasn't married. Her only question wasn't why or if, but how this could happen. She simply wanted a clarification. She asked, "How will this be since I am a virgin?" The angel explained that the Holy Spirit would "come upon" her and "overshadow" her. She replied with simple faith: "I am the Lord's servant. May it be to me as you have said."

Mary could have raised a million excuses and doubts. Really, even one would have been enough to derail God's plan for her. She could have said, "But what about Joseph? What will he say when he finds out I'm pregnant? He'll probably leave me and I'll be all alone." But she didn't raise this objection. She trusted God that what he commanded he could fulfill. And she didn't ask, "What will happen when the religious leaders discover I've gotten pregnant before Joseph and I married? They'll stone me to death! Hey, we need to be reasonable about all this. Maybe we could find a better way." These and many more questions may have swirled in Mary's head at that moment, but God's clear call overwhelmed any doubts and fears. Her "yes" to him was unequivocal.

I believe God gives all of us instructions every day, but we miss many of them because our spiritual ears are clogged. We're too preoccupied with our agendas, our desires, and the demands of our lives to pay close attention to God's Spirit. God may not use angels to announce his intentions for us, but he uses the Spirit's promptings, friends' advice, the role models of those we respect, our reading of Scripture, and sermons we hear—if we'll only listen with our hearts. No, none of us will be asked to be the parent of the Messiah today, but we can fulfill God's calling just as much as Mary fulfilled hers.

The kind of calling God gives us each day might include:

- Go love that teenager who feels angry and alone.

- Invite your neighbor over for coffee so you can build a bridge with her.

- Speak a word of affirmation to the person in the office who is so critical of everything everyone tries to do.

- Install software that blocks porn sites from your computer.

- Turn off the television and read the Bible.

- Care as much about lost people as you do about the team you root for.

- Call an old friend who needs some encouragement.

- Trust God with your finances and bring your tithe to him.

- Give someone you love a hug, ask about his or her day, and take a few minutes to listen.

- Say those words that mean so much: "I'm sorry. Will you forgive me?"

- And say those other words, "I forgive you."

When we have "yes" hearts, amazing things happen in every aspect of our lives. We become more sensitive to God and to people. We take an extra second to speak words of kindness to people we used to ignore when we were distracted. And their eyes light up because they're convinced we really care. Sometimes when I read the gospels, I try to imagine the look in people's eyes when they encountered Christ. The woman caught in adultery, Jairus, Peter when he was fishing, and dozens of others. When they looked into Jesus' eyes, they saw a "yes" heart like Mary's, and they responded with love and trust. When we have that look in our eyes, many people will respond in the same way. It's a beautiful thing to see.

Some of you are reading this chapter and thinking, "Man, I give and give all the time. I've given so much I'm running on empty!" There's a difference between saying "yes" to God and saying "yes" to people. We should always respond positively to God's invitation, but we have to be more selective about reacting to every need we see. That's codependency, not discipleship. Some have said, "The need constitutes the call," but I disagree. Jesus didn't meet every need in Palestine. He listened to the Father and went where he directed him. In the same way, we have to listen carefully and say "yes" to those things that God specifically prompts us to do. If we do too much for too many, we'll experience burnout, and we'll resent those we're trying to help instead of loving them. Like Jesus, we have to know the Father's assignment and then do it with all our hearts. Jesus said that he didn't come to do his own will but to do the will of the Father. That's the model for us to follow, too.

People in business talk about "opportunity costs." When they choose one option, they discard many others that may be almost as good. There are countless good organizations in every community and service opportunities in every church, but we have to be selective. It's better to be deeply devoted to one or a few than to spread ourselves too thin and not make a dent anywhere.

When we respond with a resounding "yes" to God, even before he asks the question, what can we expect? Certainly, we step into the greatest adventure of our lives, but true adventures always involve risks. In those months before Jesus was born, I can imagine Mary pouring over Scripture to learn more of God's plan for her coming Son. Did she read that he would die to pay for mankind's sins? Yes, I'm sure she did. Did she discover that he would be ridiculed, rejected, beaten, and discarded by his own people? Yes, she read those passages, too. So part of passing the "yes" test was embracing the suffering obedience often includes. For the years of Jesus' ministry, Mary watched him heal the sick, teach the wayward, forgive sinners, and raise the dead, but she also heard people say horrible things about him. In the end, she was one of the faithful few at the foot of the cross who watched him die. Maybe she didn't grasp all of this on the day Gabriel appeared to her, but she was committed to follow through with her commitment no matter where the journey might lead. During those years, she never gave up on God's purposes, and she never jumped in to protect Jesus from the suffering he endured. She trusted God with all her heart.

Jenni has this kind of heart as a mother to our boys. Everyday, she realizes the privilege and the urgency of raising them to love and obey God. Even before they were born, she said "yes" to God and devoted herself to raise them to become young men who love God with every fiber of their souls. She is there to comfort them when they hurt, but she's determined to avoid protecting them too much. She realizes that God has a path for each of them to follow, and they'll learn from their struggles even more than their successes. Her "yes" is to God, not to their comfort and an easy life.

What do you think it means to have a "yes" heart even before God directs us? Describe what this looks like in a person's daily life.

What are some reasons we resist saying "yes" to God? Which of these do you struggle with? How are you overcoming them?

As you look at your schedule for the next 24 hours, what are some things God is asking you to be and do? How will you respond?

Jesus, today I want to say "yes" to you. Help me...

Peter
THE OUT-OF-THE-BOX TEST

> When [Jesus] had finished speaking, he said to Simon, "Put out into deep water, and let down the nets for a catch." Simon answered, "Master, we've worked hard all night and haven't caught anything. But because you say so, I will let down the nets." (Luke 5:4-5)

On two occasions in the Scriptures, Jesus told Peter to do things that were completely out-of-the-box. The first was very early in their relationship. Peter made a living by fishing. Luke tells us that he and his partners had fished all night but caught nothing. Night was the best time to fish. Now that daylight had come, they had given up and were washing their nets. Jesus stood on the shore and called out to them to put out their nets again.

Get this: a carpenter telling professional fishermen how to catch fish. And he wasn't giving them advice about fishing in a different spot the next night. Jesus told them to do something that must have seemed absurd to Peter and his crew. I can imagine that most people would have said (or at least thought), "Hey, you don't know anything about this. I'm an expert. You're not. Go home and leave the fishing to the professionals." Peter, though, didn't trust in his skills as a fisherman. He trusted in Jesus. He spoke a mild protest, but he instantly did what Jesus told him to do—and the results were amazing. The nets caught so many fish that the boat almost sank! (For anybody who loves to fish, that's a dream come true.) The moment, however, wasn't about the fish. Jesus used this out-of-the-box experience to capture Peter's heart and set him on the road to become the leader of the church.

Usually, God uses the strengths he has given us to change lives and bring honor to himself, but occasionally, he gives us an instruction that is different—opposite, in fact—from anything we've ever imagined before. The question in those moments is: will we cling to what feels comfortable, or will we listen to God and follow his leading?

The second out-of-the-box experience for Peter happened several years later after Jesus had ascended to heaven. This time, God's instructions didn't challenge Peter's strengths. They confronted his traditions. God instructed him to reach a Gentile with the gospel of grace.

The Jews always have been rightfully proud of their role as God's chosen people. God set them apart from all other tribes, tongues, and nations to represent him. He gave them his laws, and he demonstrated his presence and power over and over again. The laws God gave them dealt with every aspect of life: relationships, worship, government, and diet. The people of God were special, and their customs and culture made them different from any nation the world had ever seen.

In the early days of the church, virtually every believer was Jewish. The eleven disciples were Jews, those who came to Christ when Peter preached at Pentecost were Jewish pilgrims, the lame man who was healed at the temple was a Jew, and the first leaders of the church were all Jewish. One of the most astounding conversions in those days was when Saul, who had captured and killed Christians, met Jesus on the road to Damascus and became a follower. When we look at Peter's response to the vision God gave him to reach a Gentile with the gospel, we need to understand that he had every reason—culturally, religiously, and ethnically—to say "no" to God's directive. But eventually, he said "yes." He learned again that God sometimes calls us to do things that are out-of-the-box.

I appreciate traditions. In our spiritual lives, they give us stability, and they remind us of how the Lord has worked in the past. Sometimes, though, we restrict the Spirit's work by holding too tightly to the way things have always been. When we're too tied to the way things have always been, we're not open to the Spirit's new directions.

We all can think of reasons and excuses for saying "no" to God at any point in our lives. We may find obedience to be too threatening, or we may think it's just inconvenient to do what God has told us to do. When he tells us to forgive someone who has hurt us, it feels much better to harbor resentment and delight in thoughts of getting back at that person. Or when God puts a needy person in front of us, we can think of a dozen excuses why it's somebody else's responsibility to stop and help. After all, we're just too busy. Some of the most insidious excuses, though, are religious ones. We don't help people of other denominations or faiths because they're "not one of us." That was Peter's perspective.

Cornelius was an officer in the Roman army, and the Romans weren't exactly welcomed guests in Palestine. They were conquerors, and the Jews hated their intrusion and intimidation. Cornelius, though, wasn't an average soldier. He loved the God of the Jews. He led his family in worship, and he gave generously to the poor. One day, in the middle of the afternoon (so Cornelius knew he wasn't dreaming), an angel appeared to him and instructed him to send some men to Joppa to find a man named Peter.

At noon the next day as the men approached the house where Peter was staying, he was hungry and went to the roof to pray while lunch was being prepared. On the roof, God gave Peter a vision. He saw a sheet lowered from heaven with both kosher and forbidden animals, reptiles, and birds. A voice told him, "Get up, Peter. Kill and eat." Everything in Peter recoiled at the order. As a good Jew, he had remained pure his whole life with respect to dietary laws, and he sure wasn't going to disavow his treasured traditions just because some strange vision told him to eat forbidden food. He instantly responded, "Surely not, Lord! I have never eaten anything impure or unclean" (Acts 10:14).

God's voice explained, "Do not call anything impure or unclean." A second sheet and voiced instructions didn't convince Peter, so God dropped the sheet again and told him a third time to eat. While Peter wondered if this was the Lord or the result of last night's pizza, the men sent by Cornelius arrived at the house. To make it really clear to Peter, the Spirit told him that the men at the door had come to see him. When Peter met the men, they told him about Cornelius and the angel's command to find him in Joppa. Finally, Peter realized that God had been speaking to him in the vision, directing him to do something outside the traditions of his faith.

The next day, Peter and a few friends followed them to Cornelius' house in Caesarea. When he heard Cornelius' story, Peter connected the rest of the dots, and he replied, "I now realize how true it is that God does not show favoritism but accepts men from every nation who fear him and do what is right. You know the message God sent to the people of Israel, telling the good news of peace through Jesus Christ, who is Lord of all" (Acts 10:34-36).

Peter explained the gospel to them, and they trusted in Jesus as their Savior. The Holy Spirit came on everyone in the house, and Peter and his friends were amazed that the gift of the Spirit had been given to Gentiles. About two thousand years before, God promised Abraham to make a great nation through him, but even more, to bless all the people on earth through Abraham. For all those years, the Jews hadn't reached out very much to other nations to share the grace of God with them. This was a pivotal moment. God had to overcome Peter's narrow view of what was acceptable and prod him to reach out to those some considered to be totally unacceptable to God.

Years before, Peter had been fishing all night but caught nothing. Jesus appeared on the shore and told Peter to put out his net again. It was the wrong time, the wrong place, and the instruction was from a carpenter, not a fisherman, but Peter obeyed. The real miracle that day wasn't that the nets became full of fish, but that Peter trusted Jesus instead of relying on his skills and knowledge as a fisherman. Now, years later, the stakes aren't just about Peter, but about all the Gentiles on the earth. Because Peter had learned to trust Jesus in spite of his skills and traditions in the boat, he was prepared to trust Jesus when he had the vision of the sheet full of unclean animals.

God doesn't always give us instructions that are outside our strengths and our traditions, but he certainly does from time to time. If we aren't open to him in those moments, we step on the hose and constrict the flow of the Spirit in our lives, and we miss out on some of the most incredible things God wants to do in us and through us.

A few months ago, the leaders of our church were talking about Peter obeying Jesus instead of trusting his own skills as a fisherman and instead of following the narrow traditions of his faith. One of our elders, Jack Mourning, observed that in the boat and with Cornelius, Peter had to see beyond what was comfortable and normal to grasp the bigger picture of God's work. He said it would be like God telling a real estate developer to hold an open house at 2:00 in the morning. It just doesn't make sense, but when people come in with checkbooks in hand, he would see a real miracle in action.

Our skills, traditions, and ability to think rationally are all strengths God builds into us, but we need to trust him more than we trust these things. If we stay locked into the way things have always been, we may feel more comfortable and less threatened, but we'll miss out on some of the most glorious adventures of walking with God.

What are some of your skills that God has used to provide for your family and touch people's lives? What are some traditions you've valued and played a role in developing your character?

How do you know when you're clinging too tightly to your strengths and your traditions instead of listening to God?

What "out-of-the-box" thing do you think God could be calling you to do? Is it attractive to you? Why or why not?

Father, I don't want to say "No" to you because I'm too tied to the way I've always done things. Today, help me...

John the Baptist
THE EGO TEST

To this John replied, "A man can receive only what is given him from heaven. You yourselves can testify that I said, 'I am not the Christ but am sent ahead of him.' The bride belongs to the bridegroom. The friend who attends the bridegroom waits and listens for him, and is full of joy when he hears the bridegroom's voice. That joy is mine, and it is now complete. He must become greater; I must become less." (John 3:27-30)

On the playground, we get a good glimpse of human nature. A child on the slide calls out, "Mommy, Mommy, watch me!" Another one yells, "Daddy, look at me hang upside down!" Whether we're 5 or 95, we long to be recognized. That's not a tragic flaw. God created us for relationships full of love and respect. We thrive on being accepted by God and by the people we love. The problem comes in this case (and in every other area of our lives) because sin distorts, clouds, and poisons God's good design. Instead of enjoying recognition, we demand to be the center of attention. Our insecurity is fed by our chief fear: rejection. And our response is to call attention to ourselves by pleasing people to win approval, proving ourselves by our accomplishments, or perhaps, giving up and hiding to eliminate any risk of rejection.

All of us face the ego test to see who is going to be in the spotlight. Do we demand that we get the attention, or do we delight in shining the light on Christ and others? One of the best examples of someone who passed the crucial ego test was John the Baptist.

John was a strange duck. He lived in the desert, dressed in burlap, and ate bugs and wild honey. (I don't imagine that he blow-dried his hair every day either!) Even though he was odd, he held a position of high esteem in the community of faith. He was a prophet, and people from far and wide came to him for wisdom and the promise of forgiveness. In spite of his popularity, John never felt obligated to soften his words. He looked people in the eye and told them to repent. Leaders with a clear, uncompromising message become a watershed in their communities. Some people follow them, but some revile them. That was true of those who listened to John. By the time Jesus came on the scene, John was perhaps the most revered spiritual leader in Palestine. For that reason, he had the most to lose when the crowds started following Christ.

But that was precisely John's goal in life. He knew that God's calling wasn't for him to be the center of attention. All of his fame, all of his prestige, and all the honors he had received were for one reason only: to be a platform for Christ to receive as much honor and attention as possible.

In a pivotal scene in the Apostle John's account of the life of Christ, some of John the Baptist's followers were concerned because "everyone is going to" Jesus. In other words, Jesus was taking John's place as the most popular leader in the land. This was a crucial moment for John and for those who followed him. If he insisted on staying in the spotlight, people would have been confused, and a division would have split the spiritual community. John, though, spoke with crystal clarity: "My life," he told them, "isn't about me at all. I live to honor Christ." In a statement of the transfer of honor, he said, "He must become greater; I must become less." John wasn't referring to his identity or to "worm theology" that he was scum. He knew that God loved him and had made him part of his family. There's no scum in that! But as a member of God's family, his task was to step out of the temporary role as leader so that people would see Jesus in all of his glory. Voluntarily stepping out of the spotlight and shining the light on someone else is the supreme ego test, and John passed with flying colors.

The more secure we are in God's love and acceptance, the more willing we are to drop our demands for attention and spend our energies honoring Christ. At times, we have to make hard choices to honor him instead of ourselves, but we get the most joy in life when we take our proper position as *holders of the spotlight* instead of insisting on *being in the spotlight*. John said his role was like the friend of the bridegroom who is thrilled to see his friend honored at his wedding. John said, "That joy is mine, and it is now complete." John's perspective flies in the face of human nature. Even as adults, many of us are like the little kids on the playground hoping someone will pay attention to us and who are thrilled to watch us perform. But John's joy wasn't in being the focal point. He was genuinely thrilled to make Jesus the focal point of people's attention and affection.

Many centuries ago, a spiritual leader observed stages in a growing believer's walk with God. The first stage is God making much of us. We become convinced of his amazing love, forgiveness, and power, and we're overjoyed to be his children. We delight in being in the spotlight of God's grace. In the second stage, God shapes us so that we learn to use our talents and gifts to touch people's lives. Here, our focus begins to shift from ourselves to others as we grow stronger and deeper in our relationship with God. The spotlight then is on our God-given gifts and usefulness. In the third stage, we find our greatest delight in giving, not getting. We are amazed that God would use us, and we consider it our highest privilege to shine the spotlight on Christ so that others see him and love him. That's the stage John the Baptist was in. Does this mean that we don't want God to be honored in the first two stages? No, but it means our devotion is deeper and our motives stronger in the third stage. I'm afraid that many believers never get to the third stage in their pursuit of God. Temptations, doubts, and distractions threaten to knock us off the path. The Scriptures are full of warnings to stay on the road, no matter how rocky it may be. Paul wrote the Corinthians (who fell off the road over and over again), "But I am afraid that just as Eve was deceived by the serpent's cunning, your minds may somehow be led astray from your sincere and pure devotion to Christ" (2 Corinthians 11:3).

Today, what floats my boat and revs my engines isn't the praise I receive. I get really excited when I see God at work to change people's lives. And I really get a kick out of watching people I lead take bold steps of faith to risk it all and trust God for great things. Even if things don't work out perfectly, their faith in action thrills my heart. I get more joy out of their success than I do from my own. I enjoy being a hero-maker instead of being the hero. I think that's what John the Baptist was talking about.

John was very clear about his assignment from God: he was called to be a forerunner of the Messiah. When people asked if he was the Messiah, he instantly told them, "No, I'm not the one, but he's coming. Be ready for him." But John not only understood his assignment, he accepted it. Some of us, especially in the early stages of spiritual growth, resist any thought of being Number 2. We still want to be in the spotlight, and we consciously or subconsciously want to bump Christ out of the light so it can shine on us. When the man came to John and said, "Hey, you've been the Big Kahuna, but people are following Jesus now," the implied question was, "Aren't you upset about that?" No, John wasn't upset at all. That's his very purpose in life, and it brought him the greatest joy imaginable. If we're not clear about our assignment and if we don't accept it gladly, we'll use ministry to win acclaim and appear to be humble so that we can gain more attention. If you think that can't happen to you, think again. It's human nature, and all of us wrestle with pride in seasons of our lives. We won't win the struggle, though, if we don't realize our assignment is to honor Christ above all else, or if we refuse to embrace that role.

The ego test is full of daily choices. If our perspective is right, our prayers will be full of praise for God—instead of asking him to bless us so we'll look successful to others. Oh, we ask for his blessing, but when he works, we will be quick to honor him instead of ourselves. Those who insist on staying in the spotlight want to use God for their own purposes, like Simon the sorcerer (in Acts 8) who offered money to buy the Holy Spirit's power. Does that sound harsh? We need to examine our hearts and see if and how much that indictment is true for us. It certainly is a temptation for me and for every other believer I know.

Proudly insisting on being the center of attention falls short of God's design for us, but false humility also misses the mark. When someone speaks powerfully, leads well, or sings beautifully and receives a compliment, I've heard some of them say, "Oh, it wasn't me. It was the Lord." When I've put myself down in false humility, I was just fishing for compliments so someone would contradict me and say, "Oh Scott, you were terrific!" I understand the lure of false humility, but we need to recognize that God works in us and through us, not around us or in spite of us. He has given us abilities, talents, and spiritual gifts to invest in his cause. When we exercise those resources, he is thrilled! For years, I thought it was more spiritual to respond to compliments with self-deprecating language, but now I simply say, "Thank you," and silently pray, "Lord, I'm so grateful for the privilege of you using me." I'm only fulfilling the assignment God has given me to bring glory to him.

Most of us serve God in support roles, far from the spotlight and the stage, but every assignment is crucial in the kingdom. Those who work in the nursery enable parents to hear God's word and respond to his grace. People who direct traffic in the parking lot are the first smiling faces a visitor sees. Those who walk over to talk to a neighbor, those who take a meal to a shut-in, and those who comfort a grieving friend are all fulfilling their God-given assignment just as much as I am when I'm preaching on Sunday morning. Everyone counts.

Over the years, I've read about Truett Cathy, the founder of Chic-fil-A, and his sons as they run the company. Together, this family and their staff work hard to provide the best environment for their employees and the best chicken sandwiches for their customers. Everything they do is dedicated to God, and their commitment to him shows up in every relationship and every corporate decision. They have received countless accolades for the quality of their business operations, but they never waver in their understanding of why they do what they do. It's all for the glory of God. They work hard, and they're thankful for the praise they receive, but they deflect every bit of honor to the one who deserves to be in the spotlight. They don't resent Jesus being the center of attention. Their purpose, their calling, and their delight is to bring attention to Christ. They, like John the Baptist, are passing the ego test.

How does a person's insecurity often result in him or her demanding to be in the spotlight?

What is your current assignment from God? How much have you embraced it and accepted being Number 2?

In what areas of your life do you struggle with wanting to be recognized and praised? How has that desire gotten in the way of God's plan and calling for your life?

Who do you know who is most like John the Baptist and delights to honor Christ? Today, what are some ways you can shine the spotlight on Christ instead of yourself?

Jesus, you deserve to be in the spotlight. Today I want to...

Jairus
THE DISAPPOINTMENT
TEST

While Jesus was still speaking, someone came from the house of Jairus, the synagogue ruler. "Your daughter is dead," he said. "Don't bother the teacher any more." (Luke 8:49)

Disappointment comes in many forms: being ignored by a friend, taken for granted by a spouse, bad news from the doctor, failing (again), and a hundred other painful moments. For me, one of the most nagging sources of disappointment is when God delays answering my prayers. I hate delays. I resent it when I get behind somebody in the drive-thru at the bank, and three cars go through in the next line before the guy in front of me finishes and drives away. He may have taken only two or three minutes, but that's more than my internal clock allotted for him!

One of the most poignant moments of disappointment in the Bible is in the life of a synagogue ruler named Jairus. His role was central to community life. He was both mayor of the town and pastor of the local house of worship. Most of the religious people we see in the gospels resented the popularity of Jesus, the itinerant preacher. Jairus, though, didn't have the luxury of standing back and condemning Jesus. He needed him because his daughter was dying. Undoubtedly, he had heard that Jesus had healed people in other cities, so when he came to his town, Jairus did something few religious leaders were willing to do: he went to Jesus, fell on his knees in front of the crowd, and asked for help.

Jesus agreed to go with Jairus to his house, but on the way, a woman who had been sick for 12 years reached past the people in front of her and touched the hem of his coat. Jesus felt power flow from him to the woman to heal her, so he stopped to talk to her. In Luke's account, we get only a glimpse of this conversation, but it must have gone on for a while because it says, "While Jesus was still speaking. . . ." Don't forget where Jesus was going. There was a very sick little girl who desperately needed his care, but he had stopped for, it seemed to Jairus, an eternity.

At that moment, someone from Jairus' house hurried to the scene and told him the news he had dreaded hearing: "Your daughter is dead. Don't bother the teacher any longer." In other words, it's over. There's no hope any more. You have to face the facts now that your beloved little girl died—because Jesus stopped to talk for such a long time with someone else. If I had been Jairus at that moment, I would have been shattered by my disappointment that Jesus didn't come through for my daughter and me.

From Jairus' perspective, it didn't make any sense at all. He was a respected religious leader; she was just a woman, and women had no standing in that culture. He was wealthy, which was a sign that God had blessed him; she had spent all her money on doctors and was now destitute, which people interpreted as God withdrawing his hand of blessing. His daughter was critically ill; the woman was chronically ill. Any ER doctor knows that in triage, medical professionals take critically ill patients before they treat those who are chronically ill.

At the second Jairus heard the bad news, his waiting seemed wasted. But all of our reasoning during times of waiting isn't a problem to Jesus.

He looked at Jairus and told him, "Don't be afraid; just believe, and she will be healed." If I had been Jairus, I might have been so overwhelmed with anger and self-pity that I would have told Jesus, "Hey, you had your chance, and you blew it! I'm going home to bury my daughter." But that's not how Jairus responded to the disappointment of delay. He went with Jesus, and Jesus raised his beloved daughter from death to life.

Jordan is a dynamic young leader I met when he moved to Texas a few years ago. In fact, he's one of the most outgoing, personable, fun-loving people I know. He is so positive and charismatic that most people would never suspect he endured gut-wrenching trauma earlier in his life. He grew up in a family that went to church, but when he was 12, his parents divorced, throwing the lives of everyone in the family into turmoil. His mom quit going to church and tried to fill the hole in her heart by partying, eventually losing everything—her car, her home, and eventually even her apartment.

When he was 15, Jordan came home one day after school to find men moving furniture into a truck. The apartment was empty, except for one box of his belongings and a note from this mother. It read: "I'm sorry, I can't afford to keep doing this. I have to do my own thing. I'm sorry for my failures as a mother. I have to be gone for a while."

Jordan thought his mother was going to be away for a couple of days, or maybe a couple of weeks, but it turned into years. In those first few days, he didn't know where to go. For three months, he lived in the locker room of the school gym, sleeping on benches or on the roof. When the school officials found him after classes had dismissed, he began living with other families from the school for several months at a time until he graduated high school.

Day after day, Jordan's world was rocked by deep disappointment. He longed for a strong, loving relationship with his mom and dad, but both had deserted him. He wanted friends who respected him, but his lifestyle was the subject of laughter or pity. Hoping to earn the respect he craved, Jordan enlisted in the United States Marine Corps after graduation. During boot camp, he excelled in every area of training, quickly getting the attention of his superiors. After boot camp, he was sent to San Diego to complete training before deployment to Iraq.

During this time Jordan got an infection, but for several reasons, he didn't receive adequate medical attention. As the condition worsened, his ability to perform declined, and he became the laughingstock of his company. Suddenly, instead of being honored and respected for his exemplary abilities, he was ridiculed as a failure. The strain proved too much to bear. The heartbreak of deep disappointment led to a psychological disorder that ended in a failed suicide attempt and a six-month stay in Balboa Psychiatric Hospital. Ultimately, he was discharged from the United States Marine Corp.

Jordan returned home still looking for the respect and acceptance he had sought since high school. In a last ditch effort to salvage his life, he headed to Texas with the promise of a job. On the way, he began a conversation with a God who he thought had walked out on him and his family years before. Through the timely call of a friend and the perfect wording of a song on the radio, Jordan began to hear the clear voice of God calling to him. At that moment he responded to the Lord, and his life changed forever. He drove to Texas reconciled to God, with a bright future ahead of him.

Since that time, Jordan has watched God's grace, love, and wisdom turn years of disappointment into strength and peace. Jordan soon became an active member at our church, enrolled and graduated from a Christian university with a pastoral degree, and got married. He and his wife Jessica currently own a business in Austin, Texas, where they are actively involved in ministry as they continue to pursue God's will.

All of us face disappointments of different kinds and at different times. I believe God whispers to us in our disappointment. Like Jairus centuries before, Jordan listened to the voice of Christ and responded in faith, and God gave him a fresh way to look at life.

Waiting is one of the most challenging tasks for believers, especially in our day when technology and communications cause us to expect every desire to be met immediately. Delays are some of the most common causes of disappointment, but when God delays, he often teaches us the most important lessons in our lives: that he's God and we're not, and we can trust him to work in his way on his schedule.

We may wait on the Lord for many different reasons: for a wayward child to come home, for medicine to reverse the impact of a disease, to get pregnant, to get pregnant again, to see a marriage restored, for wisdom about financial decisions, for direction for a career, and countless other important issues we face. Sometimes, we wait on God because we desperately want him to touch a life, and sometimes we wait for him to fulfill a clear promise. Two people who had to wait a long, long time for God to fulfill his promise were Abraham and Sarah. God promised to give them a son. At the time, they were 75 and 65 years old. I'm sure they thought they'd get pregnant very quickly because they were so old, but God had other plans. For 25 long years . . . nothing. No, that's not quite accurate. In the middle of that time, Sarah became so upset about God's delay that she decided to find her own way to accomplish the task. She sent her maid into Abraham's bedroom so she could have a child. "That'll do it," she thought. But it wasn't God's plan at all. When we try to make God hurry or circumvent his path to shorten the process, we almost inevitably cause disastrous results. Hagar and her child Ishmael caused heartache and division in the family, and we're still seeing the consequences of this bitterness in the conflict between Arabs and Jews today.

When we endure disappointment, our minds drift to places we couldn't have imagined before. Sarah became so distraught that she sent her maid to have sex with Abraham. We may think that's insane, but some of us do things just as odd because we're desperate for God to work according to our schedule. I love the interaction between Jesus and Jairus in the minute after Jairus heard the report about his daughter's death. Jesus didn't explain everything he planned to do. He just looked at him and said, "Don't be afraid; just believe." That's the moment of choice for Jairus. He held tight to the trustworthiness of Jesus in spite of his anger, in spite of his disappointment and grief, and in spite of the fact that his daughter's death had already occurred. He believed, and he courageously pointed his feet toward his house to walk with Jesus.

When we demand that God get on our schedule, we're trying to control him instead of trusting him. To the extent we believe—in the depths of our souls—that God is loving, good, and strong, we'll trust patiently and expectantly in the Lord. When he delays, we won't shake our fist at him and blame him for not coming through. We'll humbly say, "Lord, you know best. I trust you to work whenever your time is right."

How trustworthy is God? During delays, that's a question we have to consider, perhaps every day. The measure of God's grace is the cross. In his letter to the Romans, Paul outlines the grand plan of God to redeem and restore people to a relationship with him. Then he asks, "What then, shall we say in response to this?" His answer comes in the form of a rhetorical question and a strong statement. He writes, "If God is for us, who can be against us? He who did not spare his own Son, but gave him up for us all—how will he not also, along with him, graciously give us all things?" (Romans 8:31-32)

Are you waiting on God to "graciously give you" something? You probably are. Waiting is a common spiritual discipline for all of us, in every stage of spiritual growth and in every part of life. How sure can you be that God will answer in a way that is the very best (though not necessarily the way you wanted)? The cross is our assurance of God's good intentions for us. If God would give his own Son to die for us, we can be confident he'll give us everything else we need. Courage and confidence then will replace our disappointment.

Abraham and Sarah waited for 25 long years for God to fulfill his promise. Jairus waited a much shorter time, but Christ's delay caused him enormous anxiety and pain. Whether we wait for a long time or a short time, our task is to glue our hearts to his and trust him to work—

however he chooses and whenever he wants—because we trust that he is good.

One of the most familiar passages about waiting on God is in Isaiah. He wrote, "But those who hope in [or wait for] the Lord will renew their strength" (Isaiah 40:31). The Hebrew word for *waiting* means "to intertwine" or "to weave." The word *renew* means "to change clothes." As we wait, God wants us to bond with him, to grow deeper in our relationship with him and love him more than ever. So the verse means this: those who bond with God will exchange their best for his best, and they'll receive the strength, ability, and provision to do what God calls them to do. Sometimes as we wait, God enables us to fly like eagles; sometimes we run tirelessly to keep fulfilling our calling; and sometimes, the load is so heavy that it takes all of our faith in God's love and power for us to take the next step without falling down. All of these are miracles of waiting, and they enable us to trust God instead of giving in to crushing disappointment.

What are some disappointments you've endured? How well did you trust God's goodness, wisdom, and purpose during these times?

During times of delay, we're tempted to give up and take things into our own hands. What are some examples of things people do when they give up on God because he's taken too long?

What truths about God's character give you perspective and hope during times of disappointment? What difference will meditating on these truths make in your life?

In what past situations has God come through when you were ready to give up? How can remembering these moments help you trust God in the future?

Father, I want to trust you during times of disappointment. Today, help me...

The Rich Young Ruler
THE HEART-OF-THE-MATTER TEST

Jesus looked at [the rich young ruler] and loved him. "One thing you lack," he said. "Go, sell everything you have and give to the poor, and you will have treasure in heaven. Then come, follow me." At this the man's face fell. He went away sad, because he had great wealth. Jesus looked around and said to his disciples, "How hard it is for the rich to enter the kingdom of God!" (Mark 10:21-23)

I believe all of us have that "one thing" that we cling to more than anything else. It's the thing that's hardest to surrender to God because it means so much to us. For Abraham, it was his son Isaac. The old dad put his son on the throne of his heart, pushing God out of the way. To get his heart right again, God went for the jugular. Quite often, he treats us the same way. He points out the one thing that is competing with him for our affections, and he tells us to put it in its place. Sometimes it's a person, sometimes it's power or prestige or a position, and sometimes it's our possessions. God loves us too much to let us continue to wander in our selfishness in the wrong direction. He says, "I love you, and it's time to do something about the idol in your heart."

For us, the idol isn't a fetish from another religion. We're not worshipping statues or bowing down to graven images in a temple. No, the things that get in the way of God in our lives are often the most precious gifts he has given us—like Abraham's promised son, the people we love the most, talents we use to touch people's lives, our prestige, or money and possessions we enjoy.

Mark tells us that a wealthy young leader ran up to Jesus and fell on his knees in front of him. He's not shaking his fist at God, and he's not distant and aloof. He's worshipping! But his first statement reveals his heart. He says, "Good teacher, what must I do to inherit eternal life?"

Jesus, I think, was amused by the way the man addressed him. The man was on his knees, but he didn't recognize Jesus as the Messiah at all. He was holding Jesus at arm's length. Jesus responded with a question, "Why do you call me good? No one is good—except God alone." But Jesus didn't argue with him about his label. He repeated the well-known requirements of faith, and the man replied, "Been there. Done that." With piercing perception, Jesus looked into his heart and pointed out the idol that prevented him from fully following God. Without a hint of condemnation, but only as a gracious invitation, Jesus looked into his eyes and told him, "One thing you lack. Go, sell everything you have and give to the poor, and you will have treasure in heaven. Then come, follow me."

Jesus didn't shake his fist at the man, and he didn't warn him of impending doom if he didn't repent. He simply spoke the truth with grace and love, and he let the man respond however he chose. Mark tells us the man was "very sad" to hear Jesus' invitation, and he walked away. To him, money was more important than God's favor. The man, though, wasn't the only one who was sad that day. I'm sure Jesus felt sorrow as he watched him walk away.

Some people read this passage and conclude that God commands all of us to give everything away, but that's not the message in Jesus' encounter with this man. Jesus always tailored his message to each person, speaking to their hopes and dreams, as well as their hurts and dreads. His words to Nicodemus were different than those he spoke to the woman at the well, but in every encounter with people, he invited people to turn from substitutes and counterfeits to follow the real thing. Jesus knew that his men probably thought this encounter with the wealthy young man was a very awkward moment. They thought this guy was ready to be one of them, a committed follower, but Jesus knew there was an idol in his heart. As they watched the rich man walk away, Jesus turned to his men and said, "How hard it is for the rich to enter the kingdom of God!"

Was Jesus talking only about rich people? No, I think he was using the issue in this man's life to point out that all of us have something that we want to cling to, to trust in, and to give us identity. For rich people, it's often money; for parents, it's their children; for artists, it's their creative skill; and for all of us, it's whatever promises to fill our lives with pleasure and security. For many years, God may not shine his light on those things. He lets us wander along with "two minds" and "competing hearts," but if we're really serious about following him, sooner or later the bright light of his love points out the one thing that competes with his rightful place in the center of our hearts.

Certainly, there are evil desires and behaviors that take God's place in the lives of some of us. Addictions, compulsions, bitterness, and secret sins derail a person's love and loyalty to God. Most of the people I know who struggle with these things are quick to admit these evils are ruining their lives. They may wrestle mightily with the process of coming clean and experiencing God's mercy and power, but they know they've got a problem that needs to be licked.

Many of us, though, have socially acceptable sins of greed, ladder climbing, pride in a relationship, or an insatiable thirst for approval. Others look at us and marvel at our abilities and our commitments, and we cloak our pursuits in God-talk. When any person, pursuit, or possession takes God's rightful place of prominence in our lives, those things become a hindrance instead of a gift. When we use God's gifts for self-promotion, our thirst for approval and applause becomes an idol. When that happens, it's time to make an adjustment—maybe a major adjust-ment. The problem is that we don't want to change. Everything in us cries out that we deserve this thing or that honor, or we'll die if we can't devote our lives to that person. But it's time for radical surgery. Though he held the knife over his son, Abraham was willing to put himself under the surgeon's spiritual blade, and he was delivered from the cancer in his soul. In contrast, the rich young ruler refused the care of the physician.

A friend named Brian Woods told me a fascinating story of how God captured his life. He said, "Scott, I was a strong Christian: I went to church, I served, I even started my own ministry, but I was doing it all in my own strength and in my own way. I was doing good things, but I was doing them to prove myself to people around me, not to honor God. That all changed four years ago when I had a wreck that nearly took my life. I was driving down the road at 80 miles an hour multi-tasking instead of paying attention to my driving. I drifted over to the shoulder of the road and plowed into an eighteen-wheeler that had parked in a construction zone. A witness at the scene told the police that I ran into the truck without even swerving or touching the brakes. I was so badly injured that I was in a comma for 23 days. When I woke up, the healing process wasn't over. In fact, it had just begun. I got out of the hospital a few weeks later, but I couldn't go back to work for 18 months. All I could do was lie on the couch—useless. Every day for weeks, I faked like everything was okay until my kids left for school and my wife went off to work. As soon as they left and I was alone in the house, I began to yell and scream at God, cursing at him, asking him what he was do-ing. Over and over again, I yelled, 'Where is your goodness, God? Why would you do this to me after everything I've done for you?' "

After about three weeks of anger and pride-filled defiance, the lights of insight came on in Brian's heart. He explained what happened: "God spoke to me. He said, 'Brian, I love you, but you don't need me any-more.' I felt confused, so I asked him, 'God what do you mean? Of course I need you. Without you, I'll go to hell.' God said it again, 'Brian

I love you so much, but you don't need me anymore.' And it was through that 'couch process' that God began to do the deep work of changing my heart. For the first time, I saw my desperate need for God in my life."

As he related this conversation with God, Brian looked me in the eyes, and with tears coming down his face, he said, "God's grace is so great to me. If he hadn't put me on my back on that couch, I probably would've gone my whole life missing what God was trying to say to me. I thank God for his grace and his goodness toward me—that he would go to such great lengths to reach me." But Brian would be quick to point out that we don't have to wait until God allows a cataclysmic event into our lives to bring change. We can do some preventative maintenance on our hearts so we respond more quickly and avoid the pain caused by insisting on our own path.

(Let me offer this side note: Isn't it odd that we can be texting on our cell phones and driving 80 miles an hour on the highway, and yet we blame God for the wreck? We may spend more than we make, rack up debt on our credit cards, get behind on our mortgage payments, and then blame God because the bank is foreclosing on our house. We may have secret sex sins, selfish prideful attitudes, and stubbornness, and yet we're mad at God and our spouse because our marriage is falling apart. Here's the truth: God isn't responsible for all the dumb things we do and the consequences for those dumb things, but he is so loving, wise, and powerful that he will even use our worst mistakes to teach us life's most valuable lessons and bless us—if we'll trust him.)

Sometimes I imagine standing before God and saying, "Lord, I'm yours. Is there anything or anyone that's getting in the way of my relationship with you?" And I stop and listen. The temptation for me is to do what I do for the praise of people. I secretly want to be known as a great leader, a holy man God uses to transform lives. This desire is a strong temptation, but I know the devastation of letting this desire for power and prestige control me. I've seen the destruction too often in other leaders' lives. When I ask God to shine his light in my heart and show me anything that is getting in the way, I'm not surprised when he points to a self-seeking thought, an attitude, or a perspective that causes me to want too much acclaim.

We may be able to fool a lot of people about the condition of our hearts, but we can't fool God. He sees into the hidden crevices and knows our secret motives. We can resist God's light and live a lie, or we can invite God's light into our hearts and become partners with him. In one of his most powerful and beautiful psalms, King David pleaded with God,

"Search me, O God, and know my heart;

Test me and know my anxious thoughts.

See if there is any offensive way in me,

And lead me in the way everlasting" (Psalm 139:23-24).

Don't be shocked when God shows you anxious thoughts and offensive ways when you invite him to show you what's in your heart. He delights in our abject honesty and our obedience—even our reluctant obedience. I think Jesus would have been thrilled if the rich young ruler had responded like the confused man who came to Jesus and said, "I believe. Help me with my unbelief!" He's glad to help. We only need to ask him for it.

What are some things, people, or positions that can threaten to replace God on the throne of your heart?

How do you know when these things—either reprehensible secret sins or socially acceptable strengths, people, and God's good gifts—have taken God's place in our lives?

Take some time to make David's prayer your own. Listen and respond to whatever he points out.

Jesus, I want to be more like Abraham than the rich young ruler. Show me...

The Man at the Pool
THE EXCUSES TEST

Some time later, Jesus went up to Jerusalem for a feast of the Jews. Now there is in Jerusalem near the Sheep Gate a pool, which in Aramaic is called Bethesda and which is surrounded by five covered colonnades. Here a great number of disabled people used to lie—the blind, the lame, the paralyzed. One who was there had been an invalid for thirty-eight years. When Jesus saw him lying there and learned that he had been in this condition for a long time, he asked him, "Do you want to get well?" (John 5:1-6)

At first glance, Jesus' question for the crippled man at the pool seems ridiculous. Who among us has been sick for years and doesn't want to get well? But in fact, many people would say "no" even when they have the chance to be strong, whole, and healthy. Many people would rather complain than take responsibility. They feel more comfortable with the painful familiar than the challenging unknown. Counselors identify a condition called "learned helplessness," which is when a person continues to believe he has no control over his life even when opportunities for change are presented. A lot of people have learned (erroneously) that they can never change. It's a trap we can escape only when our perception of life and God changes.

184

The man at the pool had been an invalid for 38 years. During all that time, he had developed a comprehensive lifestyle revolving around his health problem. Every aspect of his life was affected: where he went, his career, his relationships, and his identity. As a beggar, he had "no skills and no bills." If he responded in faith to Jesus, he instinctively understood that everything in his world would change. He would have to start taking responsibility, making hard decisions, and get a job. Being a crippled beggar may seem like a terrible life, but many people choose to remain helpless instead of taking risks in new responsibilities.

The risk of change presents itself in many different ways. We may feel comfortable in a support role. When someone asks us to take a leadership position, we face the same kind of decision the man at the pool experienced that day. Or if a person excels at work and is offered a promotion, he may not take the new job because he's so comfortable in the old position. Alcoholics, addicts, and people with any kind of compulsive behavior have to overcome inertia in recovery. The people they knew, the places they went, and the way they acted all felt familiar to them—destructive and empty, but familiar. One lady who struggled with alcohol for years commented about the lure of the familiar, "It may be hell, but at least I know the names of the streets."

Some people have been deeply wounded emotionally. Their scars haven't formed. They still have open, gaping wounds full of hurt, fear, and anger. They see themselves as victims, and this sense of identity colors everything about them. They demand that others fix their problems, and they complain bitterly if people don't come through for them in just the way they want and in the time they expect. They get up every day with a shot of adrenaline as they anticipate ways they can get back at those who hurt them.

Bitterness inevitably leads to self-pity. Self-pity may be natural and common in human experience, but it short-circuits our faith and makes us passive. Unless we address this spiritual problem, it poisons every relationship in our lives. When we wallow in self-pity, we want attention, and we expect somebody else to fix our problems. We complain and whine, waiting for someone to notice us and come to our rescue. When they don't, we have something else to complain about! Pastor John Piper, author of *Desiring God*, offers insight about the nature of self-pity. He wrote:

> "The nature and depth of human pride are illuminated by comparing boasting to self-pity. Both are manifestations of pride. Boasting is the response of pride to success. Self-pity is the response of pride to suffering. Boasting says, 'I deserve admiration because I have achieved so much.' Self-pity says, 'I deserve admiration because I have sacrificed so much.' Boasting is the voice of pride in the heart of the strong. Self-pity is the voice of pride in the heart of the weak. Boasting sounds self-sufficient. Self-pity sounds self-sacrificing. The reason self-pity does not look like pride is that it appears to be needy. But the need arises from a wounded ego, and the desire of the self-pitying is not really for others to see them as helpless, but as heroes. The need self-pity feels does not come from a sense of unworthiness, but from a sense of unrecognized worthiness. It is the response of unapplauded pride."[11]

When we make excuses for our behavior and avoid risks of change, we miss out on the adventure of following Jesus. For some of us, though, it takes tremendous courage to face the hard truth and pursue change. A friend of mine who is a pastor told me that a church elder he inherited at his new church raised a few red flags in his mind. In the first few months my friend was at the church, he noticed that the elder was a bit too close to the 16 year-old daughter of a divorced woman who attended his Sunday school class. He hugged her a little too long and hard, and in church, he sat with his arm around the girl. For a few weeks, the pastor

---

11 John Piper, *Desiring God*, (Multnomah Books, Sisters, Oregon, 1986), p. 250.

tried to explain it away, but the Spirit wouldn't let it pass. He decided to talk to the elder, and in a meeting in his office, he diplomatically said that his relationship with the girl had the appearance of impropriety. The elder exploded! He defended himself and called the pastor a "pervert." He yelled, "I'm the father figure in this girl's life, and her mother thanks me all the time for how I care about her daughter. You have some nerve accusing me of things I wouldn't think of doing!"

The pastor backed off for a while, but he kept his eye on this man and the girl. A few months later, a visiting pastor spoke at the church one Sunday morning. At the end of his message, he asked people to come to the altar if they wanted him to pray for them. The girl came forward, and as he prayed for her, he sensed the Holy Spirit tell him that something was very wrong. He called the pastor's wife over and asked the girl to tell her what was going on. In a flood of pain and honesty, she began telling the story of two years of sexual encounters with the elder. When the pastor and his wife talked later with the mother, she admitted that she had suspected something, but discounted her fears because the man was a respected leader in the church.

The next few days were a whirlwind of the girl's tears, the mother's anguish, and the elder's rage at the police and the staff of Child Protective Services. Do you see how this relates to the man at the pool? All of these people were asked, in effect, "Do you want to get well?" The pastor first offered healing to the elder in his office, but he refused. When the girl was offered hope, coupled with the risk of truth and responsibility, she said, "Yes." Her mother had many opportunities to take responsibility for her daughter's well being during those two years, but she found excuses to avoid the hard subject. Finally, though, she had the courage to confront the abuser and put a stop to her daughter's pain.

The road for the girl and her mother hasn't been easy. Years of pain, confusion, deception, fear, and anger boiled out of both of them, but their honesty was a fertile environment for God to touch their hearts—individually and together. Today, they would tell you that they learned some important lessons through the excruciatingly painful experience. The elder, however, never broke. His heart remained rock hard, and he blamed the church of falsely accusing him. A jury came to a different conclusion. As far as I know, he's still in jail.

Change—whether it's the risk associated with a job promotion, a step out of the hell of addiction or abuse, or dealing with the deep disappointment that life isn't what we hoped it would be—is never easy. We may feel more comfortable remaining where we are, but God calls us to trust him and take bold steps forward. The man at the pool picked up his mat and walked away. In his new strength and freedom, the Jewish leaders confronted him, and he simply spoke the truth about what Jesus did for him. He didn't go back to be a beggar at the pool. He kept telling people that Jesus made him well and gave him new life.

Ultimately, our response to change is a reflection of the condition of our hearts. If we live in fear, we'll insist on every question being answered and success guaranteed before we're willing to take the slightest step. If, however, we're convinced that God is good, wise, and strong, we'll trust him and move forward, even if we don't yet know all the answers.

Do you want to get well? Are you willing to take responsibility and trust God instead of remaining passive and safe? We all face these questions from time to time . . . maybe today.

What are some reasons passivity and immobility can seem so attractive?

If you had been the man at the pool, how would you have responded to Jesus?

What are some areas in your life in which you need to "get well"? What are some choices you've made recently, or that you need to make, that offer you the opportunity to "get well"?

Jesus, when you ask if I want to get well, I want to say, "Yes." Today, help me to...

The Disciples
THE COURAGE TEST

At that time Jesus said to the crowd, "Am I leading a rebellion, that you have come out with swords and clubs to capture me? Every day I sat in the temple courts teaching, and you did not arrest me. But this has all taken place that the writings of the prophets might be fulfilled." Then all the disciples deserted him and fled. (Matthew 26:55-56)

When people feel threatened, the normal reaction is to move into a self-protective mode as quickly as possible. The threats may be real or imagined, but when we sense that our lives are out of control, fight or flight may be the only options we see. At the moment of Jesus' greatest vulnerability, the disciples tried both of those avenues.

For weeks, perhaps months, Jesus had told his followers that the religious leaders wanted to kill him. After he raised Lazarus from the tomb and Passover approached, the plotters put their plans into action. The week before his arrest, Jesus didn't back down an inch. Every day, he was in the temple arguing with the rigid, legalistic leaders who felt so threatened by his message of grace and love. On that Thursday night, he ate the Passover dinner with his followers, and again, he told them he was soon to die. Later that night on a nearby hillside, they watched him pray in agony as he anticipated the suffering of the next day. Still, they didn't understand what was happening. When they saw Judas leading soldiers to arrest Jesus, Peter grabbed a sword and cut off a man's ear. (To the man's relief, Peter was a fisherman, more skilled with nets than weapons.)

When fighting didn't resolve the problem, and the soldiers arrested Jesus, the disciples turned tail and ran as fast as they could. They had watched Jesus raise the dead, heal the sick, and teach the greatest truths the world had ever heard, but in their moment of testing, they ran like scalded dogs! At the moment Jesus needed friends, they deserted him. When the test of their loyalty occurred, they valued their own skin over him. John and Peter showed up at one of the trials, but when strangers asked Peter if he knew Jesus, he denied it three times. At the cross, John was the only disciple who dared show his face to stand with the faithful, grief-stricken women.

In our lives, many things make us feel out of control, and when we have that awful feeling, we, too, want to fight or run away instead of trusting God in the middle of the problem. The Bible contains 365 instances when God, angels, or prophets tell people, "Fear not!" Why is this statement spoken so many times? Because our lives are colored so much by fear. We're afraid of losing our jobs, being passed over for a promotion, getting married and of not getting married, having children or being barren, our children drifting toward drugs and premarital sex, hearing bad news from our doctors, being misunderstood by our closest friends, not measuring up in some way, or experiencing the pangs of rejection and isolation. On a bigger scale, we feel overwhelmed by powers that seem to control our lives but over which we have absolutely no power. The government, national political parties, and financial markets do whatever they do without even asking for our advice! And we're sure there are unseen but powerful spiritual forces all around us, shaping events, causing problems, and creating hurts.

The disciples failed the courage test when they felt out of control, but Jesus passed with flying colors. None of what happened was a surprise to him, so he never felt helpless. Certainly, in the garden he dreaded the suffering that loomed large the next day, but he never doubted his Father's will or goodness. A few years ago when the movie *The Passion of the Christ* was in theaters, people asked, "Why did Jesus die?" and "Who killed Jesus?" Those are wonderful questions to discuss. The real answer, though, isn't that the Jews or the Romans killed him. He was sent to earth to die. It was the Father's grand plan of grace. No one forced anything on Jesus. He was in complete control from first to last.

When he was arrested, the scene became chaotic after Peter cut off the high priest's servant's ear. Jesus calmly reached out and put the ear back in its place and announced, "Put your sword back in its place, for all who draw the sword will die by the sword. Do you think I cannot call on my Father, and he will at once put at my disposal more than twelve legions of angels? But how then would the Scriptures be fulfilled that say it must happen in this way?" Angels were (and are) immensely powerful. It's as if Jesus was saying, "I can do anything I want to do. All the power of the universe is in my hands, but I'm not going to use it to stop what's going to happen now. In fact, dying is the very reason I came."

A few hours later, another remarkable conversation took place at the governor's palace. Historians tell us that Pilate was a vicious, bloodthirsty ruler. Anyone who crossed his path was in danger of suffering any punishment he chose, usually an excruciating death on a cross. When Jesus was dragged before Pilate, though, Jesus showed no fear in the least. Pilate announced what was obvious to everyone in the land: that he had complete power over everybody and everything. He probably snarled at Jesus, "Don't you realize I have power either to free you or to crucify you?"

Jesus calmly replied, "You would have no power over me if it were not given to you from above. Therefore the one who handed me over to you is guilty of a greater sin" (John 19:10-11). In the hour most people would feel completely out of control and severely threatened by an evil man standing in front of them, Jesus was calm and collected. He trusted that the Father had everything in his hands. The lesson is clear: Even when it looks like everything is going haywire, God is still sovereign. We can trust in his goodness, his wisdom, and his authority over all of his creation. In his last statement before he ascended back into heaven, Jesus told his followers, "All authority in heaven and on earth has been given to me" (Matthew 28:18). He still retains all authority today.

When we feel threatened and want to fight or run away from trouble, we need to realize two crucial things: *who we are* and *whose we are*. We are God's children: chosen by him before the foundations of the world, adopted, forgiven, and sealed by the Holy Spirit until the day we meet Jesus face to face. And we belong to him. He bought us with a high price, and we are no longer our own. We are inscribed on the palms of his hands, and he prays for us all day every day. In fact, we are never out of his mind, and we never stop being on his heart.

A few years ago when Dakota was a little boy, he was in the church's nursery. The childcare worker told him to do something, but he didn't want to. They argued for a few minutes, and then Dakota looked intently into her eyes and said with tremendous resolve, "Obviously, you don't know who my Daddy is!" I'm sure it wasn't appropriate for him to defy the nursery worker that day, but at another level, his attitude is a wonderful example for us. When the world wants to shape us into its mold, when the economy is collapsing, when we hear terrible news, when those we trust forsake us, or when anything else makes us feel out of control, we can stand up, look the problem in the eye and say, "You may think you can threaten me, but you don't know who my Father is! He's in complete control, and I trust him with all my heart."

Fear is probably the most common human emotion, and it reaches into the deepest crevasses in our lives. It's so pervasive in most of our lives that we can't really imagine life without it. The multitude of the

Bible's commands like "Don't be afraid" tell us that fear is common, and God wants us to be honest with him about it. In his insightful book, *Following Jesus*, N. T. Wright observes that the resurrection of Jesus speaks powerfully to our deepest fears. The power of God demonstrated by the resurrection of Jesus shatters our puny notions of God and elevates our faith in him, even in the most difficult moments of our lives. It is a deep well of courage for us in fearful times. He writes:

> "If we believe in the God who raised Jesus, then, as our fears are dealt with at a deeper level, as they are met by the astonishing love of the surpassing God, we will be able to leave behind the image of a bossy, bullying God who wants us to keep his laws in order to control us, to lick us into shape, to squash or stifle our humanness or our individuality. Instead, we will be able to follow the true God, the God who raises the dead, in trust rather than fear. The true God gives new life, deeper, richer life, and helps us towards full mature humanness, by prising [prying] open the clinched fists of our fears in order to give his own life and love into our empty and waiting hands."[12]

We don't overcome our fears by hiding until they go away or by fighting back in mindless fury. Our fears reveal our human condition. Courage doesn't mean we never fear, but that we trust God in the middle of our fears. As the psalmist prayed, "When I am afraid, I will trust in you" (Psalm 56:3). The challenge for us is to be completely honest with God about our fears, to avoid the temptation to run away or fight back, and to cling to God's goodness, wisdom, sovereignty, and power through thick and thin—and to remember who our Daddy is.

---

12 N. T. Wright, *Following Jesus*, (Eerdman's Publishing, Grand Rapids, Michigan, 1994), p. 72.

What are some ways fear (both obvious and hidden) shapes the lives of people you know?

What are some things that make you (or in the past have made you) feel out of control?

When you feel threatened, how will it help to remember who you are and whose you are?

Jesus, you met the courage test because you were so confident of the Father's goodness and his plan. Today, I want to face my fears and trust you with...

Paul
THE DIRECTION TEST

Paul and his companions traveled throughout the region of Phrygia and Galatia, having been kept by the Holy Spirit from preaching the word in the province of Asia. When they came to the border of Mysia, they tried to enter Bithynia, but the Spirit of Jesus would not allow them to. So they passed by Mysia and went down to Troas. During the night Paul had a vision of a man of Macedonia standing and begging him, "Come over to Macedonia and help us." After Paul had seen the vision, we got ready at once to leave for Macedonia, concluding that God had called us to preach the gospel to them. (Acts 16:6-10)

Many Christians feel very uneasy when they hear talk about following God's leading—not because they doubt that God leads. They feel pretty certain that God leads *other people,* but they're not sure they can discern the direction he's pointing *them* to go. They've heard countless stories about God's miraculous leading in the lives of devout believers, but they wonder if the Holy Spirit can break through the fog in their own minds to lead them, too. He can, and he will. We just have to know what we're listening to.

I love to read the stories about men and women in the Bible as they pursued God with all their hearts. The Scriptures don't paint them as "super saints," but as flawed, finite people struggling to figure out how to relate to the infinite God of the universe. God called the apostle Paul to reach every person on the planet. That was his goal, his passion, and his plan. Paul had been a very self-reliant man, tough as nails and sure of himself—until Jesus changed his heart and gave him a large dose of grace-filled humility. As he traveled to city after city, God used him to reach the lost. It's an amazing story. The guy who used to capture and kill Christians was now leading people to Christ! Luke tells us that on one of his mission trips, Paul wanted to go to a part of modern-day Turkey then called Asia, but the Holy Spirit didn't let them go there. He then set his sites on another part of Turkey called Bithynia, but the Spirit said "no" to that idea, too. Was Paul dejected? Was he angry with God? Luke doesn't mention any sense of discouragement at all. If I'd been Paul, I would have wondered why the Spirit had stopped me. Don't those people need Jesus, too? But by this time, Paul had learned to value the Spirit's nudges more than his own power of reasoning.

That night, the Lord gave Paul a vision instructing him to cross from Asia into Europe to plant the seed of the gospel on that continent. Immediately, he responded to God's clear directive, and the rest, as they say, is history.

What do we expect when God leads us clearly: smooth sailing and clear skies? That's not always (or even often) God's agenda when we follow him. It certainly wasn't for Paul and those who hung out with him on the trip. They went to Philippi and led Lydia to Christ, but soon they were arrested, whipped, beaten, and thrown into the deepest hole in the dungeon. When they sang praises instead of complaining, God caused an earthquake to shake the locks off their chains and the doors. In city after city, they spoke out boldly about Jesus, and in every location, some believed the message and some despised the messengers. Eventually, God led Paul to the political and military center of the world, Rome, where he told everyone who would listen about Christ. Time after time, Paul passed the direction test. He trusted God would lead him, listened carefully, and responded to God's instructions.

God leads us in much the same way he led Paul. The first bench-mark of God's direction is the Scriptures. God never directs us to do anything that is contrary to the Bible. Some people have insisted that God led them to commit adultery. They felt passionate about that person, and they assumed the strong feelings were a sign from God. The Scriptures, though, never lead us to lie, cheat, steal, commit adultery, or anything else branded as sin in the Bible. On the positive side, we can be sure that God delights in leading us to love God and love people. There are hundreds of clear directions and commands in the Bible. Our first stop in determining God's will is to read the book he gave us.

God may use open doors or closed doors to guide us. Open doors are opportunities to serve him and advance in different areas of our lives. Being accepted to a college, getting a job offer, or a proposal of marriage are open doors, but the fact that the door is open doesn't necessarily mean God wants us to walk through it! We still need discernment to see if this is the right door for us. Closed doors are a little easier to discern. When the college dean sends a letter that begins, "We regret to inform you," it's not a positive sign. Even then, however, it may not be the end. Sometimes God wants us to keep knocking on a door until it eventually opens. Again, we need the Spirit's guidance to know if we should take "no" for God's answer, or keep persisting.

Mature, godly people play a vital role in helping us figure out what God is doing in our lives. We shouldn't look for people who will tell us only what we want to hear. That's not a source of wisdom. I want to talk to people who have the courage and insight to tell me the truth, even if I don't want to hear it. Those are the people I trust when I'm trying to find God's direction.

Some of us would say that having a sense of peace is a sign that God is leading us, but we have to be very careful about that. The person who committed adultery might have felt a strong sense of peace that he was doing the right thing, but it was hormones, not the Holy Spirit. When Jesus prayed in the garden before he was arrested, beaten, and crucified, he felt tremendous anguish because he knew the Father's will, not because he doubted it. Most often, though, we need to pay attention when we feel a "check" in our spirits when we're considering an option. I think that's how God guided Paul away from Asia and Bithynia, and a strong sense of uneasiness is often how God gets my attention and redirects me, too.

As we learn to walk with God and grow closer to him, we develop spiritual intimacy that enables us to discern God's heart more readily. From time to time, God breaks into my consciousness and speaks a word to me, not audibly, but just as clearly as if he had been sitting in my office talking to me. This kind of closeness with God is often the result of years of fellowship with God, but it's always by grace, so it can happen at any time. I've known new believers who had the vivid experience of God speaking to them, and it confirmed their relationship with him.

On what issues can we trust God to lead us? Anything and every-thing: work, marriage, raising children, finances, service, lost friends, and everything else important to us. We shouldn't think, though, that God wants to tell us which socks to wear each morning. He doesn't get into that level of details in our lives. He leaves those things to you and me—sometimes with the help of my wife!

God's leading doesn't always happen on our timetable, and in fact, it seldom happens when we want it to. God's timing is impeccable, but he's often much slower about letting us in on his desires than we'd like. The Scriptures say a lot about waiting on the Lord, and it's a discipline most of us need to learn. As we wait, God often does a significant work in our lives to prepare us for what's to come. We shouldn't give up on God when he doesn't answer our prayers right away. He's more than able to direct us, but he may be doing something to prepare us or oth-ers first. If we trust his goodness, we'll be able to wait more expectantly and patiently. Much later, long after the fulfillment of God's designs, we may understand why God delayed his leading. Søren Kierkegaard, a theologian and philosopher, commented, "Life can only be understood backward, but it must be lived forward."

Over the years, I've learned to expect the unexpected in God's leading. Not long ago we planned a sermon series on Dr. Seuss stories. The messages had been planned for months, but one week, I sensed that God was leading me to use *The Grinch Who Stole Christmas* instead of *Green Eggs and Ham*. (Do you think Paul ever wrestled with decisions like this?) To change messages the week before a service is a monumental issue for the creative staff at our church. I'm sure they wanted to strangle me, but they graciously pitched in to make it work. After the message, I thought it went well, but I wondered why God had led me to change the topic that week. A few days later, I learned that a man had come that morning, and God had used that specific message to touch his heart. His wife had left him two years before, and he became deeply depressed and dropped out of church. Early that morning, the Spirit woke him up and told him to go to our church. He resisted, thinking it was an absurd idea, but he finally got dressed and drove into our parking lot. With a ton of misgivings, he got out, came in, and sat down. When he opened the program, it said the series was titled "Theologins for Your Noggins." This, he was now convinced, was way beyond absurd! When I started speaking that morning's message on *The Grinch Who Stole Christmas*, he almost fell out of his chair. In the past two years, he had become so sour that people where he worked started calling him "the Grinch." That morning, I explained that God's grace can save us and heal the wounds in our hearts. He can take our sick, broken, lifeless hearts and miraculously bring them back to life in him. And by the end of the message, that's exactly what happened. God touched his heart, and he found more peace, love, and joy than he could remember ever having.

During that week, I wondered what in the world I was doing changing the message. It was inconvenient to our staff, and it made me look a bit silly. But I was sure God wanted me to speak on that topic, so I did.

I'm just glad God let me see a glimpse of how he used that message to turn a Grinch into a person again.

Some of the most precious moments of my life have occurred when I listened to God's whispered directions. On my wife's grandfather's 90th birthday, the whole family went over to his house to celebrate with him and Namaw. People had talked to him about Christ for decades, but he had always said, "I can't believe something I can't see." At this point in his life, his health was failing, and I wondered how much longer he had to live. On the drive over to his house, the Holy Spirit told me, "Tonight is the night." I didn't have to ask for any clarification. I knew exactly what he meant. After dinner, cake, and presents, people began leaving. I asked, "Grandfather, do you mind if I stay around and talk with you for a while?"

He grinned and said, "I'd love that."

I then said, "Grandfather, I'd like to talk to you about spiritual things. Is that okay?"

He smiled, "Why Scott, you're my pastor! It's only right for you to talk to me about things of the Lord." Now, you have to understand that this was the first time he had ever referred to me as his pastor. He and Namaw had moved to our community about eight months earlier, and they had begun attending our church. His words and the twinkle in his eye told me that the Spirit had prepared him to hear the gospel.

Right after we began talking, Namaw must have gotten nervous. She walked in and asked, "What are you men talking about?"

Grandfather motioned with his hand for her to leave, and he told her, "Now Nancy, I'm just talking with my pastor. We'll be all right. Don't you worry about a thing."

For the next few minutes, I told him the same message people had shared with him dozens of times before. This time, however, when I asked if he understood and wanted to trust Christ as his Savior, he said, "That's what I've wanted my whole life: to know God like you know him. I just haven't known how."

I led him in the sinner's prayer, and when he looked up, the countenance of his face had changed. I assured him that he had just begun a relationship with Jesus, and that one day he'd see him face to face.

Two months later, Grandfather died. At the funeral, I told the story about the night God prepared him and directed me to have a life-changing conversation about the grace of Christ. I have many wonderful memories of Grandfather, but none I treasure as much as those moments after the party on his 90th birthday. It happened because I was willing to listen and respond to the Spirit that night. Someone took a picture of Grandfather and me at the party that night. Every time I look at it, I'm filled with gratitude for him and for God's grace in both of our lives that night.

We talk about "discipleship" as a high value for believers. It means *to follow*, a word that implies that our leader gives us directions. If we insist on our own way, we aren't good followers, or if we doubt when God leads, we won't ever take the first step. Be a willing, wise follower of Christ. It's the adventure of your life!

What are some instances when God clearly led you? Did you see the fruit of that leading immediately, later, or ever?

How can we know the difference between the Spirit's directions and our own desires?

What are some opportunities or obstacles in your life right now for which you need God's direction?

Father, I want to follow you. Today, I want to ask you for directions for...

Jesus
THE WILDERNESS TEST

Jesus, full of the Holy Spirit, returned from the Jordan and was led by the Spirit in the desert, where for forty days he was tempted by the devil. He ate nothing during those days, and at the end of them he was hungry. (Luke 4:1-2)

I'm afraid that too many of us have an unrealistic picture of Christ and of spiritual life. When we think of Jesus, we see him as the stained glass guy with a sweet smile on his face and a lamb over his shoulders. He seems plastic and unapproachable. Similarly, when we think of the Christian life, we believe "the abundant life" is effortless and carefree "with the Spirit carrying us along on the jet stream of his love." Sure, I've heard preachers say things like that. They mean well, but they may give the wrong impression of a life of faith. When people believe the Christian life should be easy, they quickly become confused and discouraged when they face difficult tests. Even Jesus, the Son of God, wasn't exempt from severe testing. His invitation, "Follow me," takes us into testing of all kinds, just like the ones he experienced.

Luke gives us the most extensive account of the birth of Christ, and he reports the beginning of his earthly ministry when John the Baptist baptized Jesus. At that moment, the heavens opened, the Spirit descended on him, and the Father's voice boomed, "You are my Son, whom I love; with you I am well pleased" (Luke 3:22). Ahh, everything's looking good, isn't it? In the very next scene, however, we find the Spirit leading Jesus into the wilderness to be tempted by Satan. In an understatement bordering on humor, Luke tells us that after fasting for 40 days, Jesus became hungry! At that moment of vulnerability, the temptations came fast and furiously. The devil's first temptation was to provide food for Jesus. Even though he was famished, he knew that God would provide the spiritual food he needed. The second offer was to rule the kingdoms of the earth—if Jesus would worship Satan. Jesus responded with single-minded devotion to worship the Father alone. The devil's third offer was more complex. He said, "If you are the Son of God, jump down" from the temple in Jerusalem. Satan assured him, "Surely the angels would catch you." He hoped Jesus would feel compelled to prove himself, but he didn't take the bait.

From this passage, we can draw many different conclusions, but I want to point to only two. First, all of us experience temptation and testing. It's not just for the weak, and it's not reserved for super-saints. Temptation is a common experience for all of us. These tests came to Jesus in three distinctly different forms, and Satan tempts us in a variety of ways, too. Second, feeling tempted isn't sin. We sin only if we give in to the temptation. The enemy of our souls wants us to feel guilty and self-condemned even when we have thoughts that threaten to draw us toward "the lust of the flesh, the lust of the eyes, and the boastful pride of life." Thoughts come in and out of our minds, but we can choose to dwell on them or not. As a shrewd person said, "We can't keep birds from flying over our heads, but we can keep them from building nests in our hair!"

Temptations, like all other tests, are watersheds in our spiritual lives. If we give in, they poison our hearts and our relationships, but if we trust God and stand strong, they prepare us for a bigger assignment in God's kingdom.

One of the biggest lies the enemy tells us is that we're completely alone in the temptation we're facing. That simply isn't true. There are people around us who will understand—not everybody, and not necessarily the ones we want to understand, but God will provide somebody who will give us support when we need it most. More than that, Jesus understands. The writer to the Hebrews tells us, "Therefore, since we have a great high priest who has gone through the heavens, Jesus the Son of God, let us hold firmly to the faith we profess. For we do not have a high priest who is unable to sympathize with our weaknesses, but we have one who has been tempted in every way, just as we are—yet was without sin. Let us then approach the throne of grace with confidence, so that we may receive mercy and find grace to help us in our time of need" (Hebrews 4:14-16).

Do you feel alone? Jesus endured loneliness, too. Have you been betrayed? His closest friends ran away when he needed them most. Do you feel misunderstood? Jesus' family members told people he was insane! Have you been ridiculed and rejected? The religious establishment viciously attacked him at every turn. Jesus has "been tempted in every way, just as we are." That doesn't mean he was tempted to use modern email to gossip about a friend, but it means that he experienced every category of temptation known to mankind—but he never gave in. Because he understands, we can go to him with any and every problem. No matter what's going on in our lives, he gets it. He understands, and he never pushes us away in disgust. At his throne of grace, we find mercy, love, and kindness.

When Christ invited us to follow him, the path eventually leads to the top of the mountain and to the barrenness of the desert. Every experience shapes our faith and gives us insight into the nature of God and the needs of people around us. If he is our example, we should expect to experience some of the same tests he endured. In his first letter, Peter wrote to people who had endured a lot of persecution for their faith. Some of them, we can surmise, were shocked at the hardships they experienced. He assured them, "Dear friends, do not be surprised at the painful trial you are suffering, as though something strange were happening to you. But rejoice that you participate in the sufferings of Christ, so that you may be overjoyed when his glory is revealed" (1 Peter 4:12-13). The point isn't popular with many television preachers, but Peter explains that "the abundant life" necessarily includes suffering. The tests of suffering enable us to identify more closely with Jesus—to feel the same kind of pain and enjoy the closeness of the Father's love in those hard times.

We don't just endure desert times once in our lives and never face temptation again. At the end of the 40 days in the wilderness, Jesus returned to Galilee "in the power of the Spirit" where he began his amazing ministry, but Satan "left him until an opportune time." Throughout his three years of ministry, Jesus endured many difficult times, but nothing could compare to those hours on the cross. There, Satan returned in force. Jesus felt abandoned by everyone, including the Father, as he bore the sins of the world. Even there, however, he didn't sink into despair and resentment. As men nailed him to the wood, he responded, "Father, forgive them, because they don't know what they're doing."

What does this mean for you and me? It means God always has a purpose for us in times of temptation, trial, and testing. These are parts of his curriculum to teach us lessons of spiritual life we can learn in no other way. In his school, there are no shortcuts, no classes to skip, and no easy promotion to the next level. But we can be assured that he is with us, he is for us, and he'll use every difficult moment to shape us a little more like Jesus. In John's gospel, Jesus explains that everyone who is fruitful is pruned like a productive grapevine so that we can bear more fruit. The pain of pruning, then, is a sure sign of God's approval, not his displeasure. It's preparation for another stage in the adventure of following and serving him.

A few years ago, I had a very unsettling dream. I dreamed I was in the church on a dark, foreboding night, and several hooded men got out of a limousine at the front door. I was sure they wanted to break in and kill me. They came to the door, shook it, and realized it wasn't open. They ran to the side door and tried to get in there, but it was locked. They tried every door in the church, and I ran through the halls to see if they got in. Finally, they realized all the doors were locked, and they left. I woke up in a cold sweat. In a few minutes, the meaning of the dream became crystal clear. Satan had been testing me to see if he could find any weak place to attack. Just as he had tempted Jesus in several ways, he was testing me in several places at once, too. I couldn't afford to let my guard down a single time. The risks were too great—for my church, for my family, and for me.

When we experience difficult times and are tempted to respond, "Lord, why me?", we can find comfort in the knowledge that we're going through the same kind of experiences Jesus endured. If we're serious about being his disciple, we can expect to enjoy the richest blessings imaginable, but we also expect to face a fair share of loneliness, rejection, misunderstanding, and accusation. Sometimes, we may think we can't make it, but God assures us that he'll never give us more than we can handle (1 Corinthians 10:13). Through them all, we have a friend who is closer than a brother, one who doesn't condemn us for being tempted, but who roots for us as our biggest cheerleader even when we feel down. Wilderness tests are part of the Christian walk of faith. They're important classes in God's school for us. We have options in how we respond. We can ignore them, resent them, or study like crazy and learn the lessons God wants to teach us. The choice is ours each day.

Why is it important to realize that temptation isn't sin?

What are some temptations you experience? How do you normally handle them? After reading today's chapter, how should you handle them?

What are some lessons God wants to teach you through wilderness tests in your life?

Jesus, I don't go through anything you didn't experience when you were on earth. Today, help me face...

The Judgment Seat of Christ
THE ULTIMATE REPORT CARD

If any man builds on this foundation using gold, silver, costly stones, wood, hay or straw, his work will be shown for what it is, because the Day will bring it to light. It will be revealed with fire, and the fire will test the quality of each man's work. If what he has built survives, he will receive his reward. If it is burned up, he will suffer loss; he himself will be saved, but only as one escaping through the flames. (1 Corinthians 3:12-15)

Many people who are young in their faith are surprised to discover there are two judgments at the end of time. One is the Great White Throne, described in Matthew 25 and Revelation 20. At this event, believers and unbelievers will be separated. Believers will enter God's presence, and those who rejected Christ will experience eternal isolation away from him and everything good. When most people think of judgment, this is the event they're thinking about. But there's another judgment, one reserved for Christians. It's called the Bema Seat or the Judgment Seat of Christ. It's not about salvation; it addresses our efforts to please God (or not) after we became Christians. Paul tells us that on a day in the future, we'll stand before Christ for the ultimate report card. All the tests we've experienced since the moment we trusted in Christ will be evaluated and graded. Everything we've done passes through a fire of judgment. For those times we trusted God with our difficulties and advanced the kingdom when God gave us opportunities, we receive a reward from God's hand. And those things that don't pass the test are burned up and forgotten.

As our Good Teacher, God let's us know what will be on this final exam. He explains that every moment of every day, every thought, word, and action in our lives as children of God will pass through the fire. Knowing what is coming gives us motivation to study hard now! In our day (like Paul's), some people look at the endless cycles of seasons and eras of history and conclude, "Things haven't changed. Christ isn't really coming back." With this assumption, they disregard God's instructions and live for themselves. But he is coming back, and we will stand before him—it may not be today, but it'll happen. We can count on it.

For every commercial airline flight, the captain provides a detailed flight plan. The plane, though, doesn't stay exactly on the flight path. Winds push it to one side or the other, and weather conditions force the pilot to fly around thunderstorms or above bumpy layers in the sky. For the entire flight, the pilot continually corrects his actual position to get back to the original flight plan. It's the same in our spiritual lives. God has given us a clear flight plan to follow. His word contains commands and promises to guide us. But we drift. The winds of distraction and discouragement sometimes blow us off course for a while, and we make daily and hourly corrections to get back on track.

At the Judgment Seat, Christ won't just evaluate our behaviors. Those are important, but following a rigid set of rules doesn't impress God if our motive is to impress people around us that we're righteous— or more importantly, more righteous than them! Our actions are very important, but God also looks at our hearts. Paul told the Corinthians, "If I speak in the tongues of men and of angels, but have not love, I am only a resounding gong or a clanging cymbal. If I have the gift of prophecy and can fathom all mysteries and all knowledge, and if I have a faith that can move mountains, but have not love, I am nothing. If I give all I possess to the poor and surrender my body to the flames, but have not love, I gain nothing" (1 Corinthians 13:1-3). Most of us know believers who do a lot of right things but have sour dispositions. As a man said about a group like this centuries ago, "They are right but repulsive." That kind of spirit doesn't impress God at all.

A man came up to Jesus and asked him an important question: "Teacher, which is the greatest commandment in the Law?" Jesus answered, " 'Love the Lord your God with all your heart and with all your soul and with all your mind.' This is the first and greatest commandment. And the second is like it: 'Love your neighbor as yourself.' All the Law and the Prophets hang on these two commandments" (Matthew 22:36-40). Loving God and loving people—these will be rewarded with gold, silver, and precious stones on that day.

God has put immortality in our hearts, and we long for our lives to really matter. Some of us get bogged down with anxiety and greed, and the seedlings of our faithfulness get choked out by the worries of the world and the deceitfulness of riches. But the promises of God ring true. Loving him and loving people for his sake is all that really matters. When we stand before him on that day, he'll ask us, "What did you do with all I gave you?" It won't work to complain that we didn't have as much as this person or that one. We don't answer for them, only for ourselves. When we see him face to face, we'll get a report card for how we used every dollar, every possession, every hour, and every talent God has given us. Paul said, "To live is Christ, to die is gain." If we understand what will be evaluated on that day, we'll have insight about living for Christ all day every day while we're still above the ground.

When we are convinced that we will stand before Christ, our all too human fear of death may subside because we'll know there's so much more than we've experienced on this side of the curtain. Like Paul, we'll be sure that "to die is gain." Theologian and author Richard John Neuhaus wrote a letter to give perspective to a man who was dying. In the letter, Neuhaus described the impact of his own near-death experience.

The spread of a tumor led to ruptured intestines and emergency surgery. As he recovered in the hospital, he had a vision of heaven. He saw two "presences" in the room with him. He wrote, "I pinched myself hard, and ran through the multiplication tables, and recalled the birth dates of my seven brothers and sisters, and my wits were vibrantly about me. The whole thing had lasted three or four minutes, maybe less. I resolved at that moment that I would never, never let anything dissuade me from the reality of what had happened. Knowing myself, I expected I would later be inclined to doubt it. It was an experience as real, as powerfully confirmed by the senses, as anything I have ever known."

Like Paul, the certainty of being with Christ after death gave Neuhaus perspective about living for him in this life. He explained, "Be assured that I neither fear to die nor refuse to live. If it is to die, all that has been is but a slight intimation of what is to be. If it is to live, there is much I hope to do in the interim."[13]

If we understand what the Judgment Seat of Christ is about, we have insight about how and why we live each day. Like Neuhaus, we won't be terrified of death, and we'll live each moment with joy and love for Christ. As I think about that day, I'm not as motivated by the crowns I'll receive. I'm far more interested in another reward: God's smile. I want to see him look at me and say, "Great job, Scott! I gave myself for you, and Scott, you gave yourself for me. That's so cool. Well done, enter into the joy of your Master!" Paul wrote again to the Corinthians about that moment: "So we make it our goal to please him, whether we are at home in the body or away from it" (2 Corinthians 5:9). The consuming passion of Paul's life wasn't to prove himself to earn God's approval. He knew his only hope was the grace of God. But as he soaked up the incredible grace, mercy, and love of Christ, his response was to say, "Lord, I'm yours, all of me all the time. Fill me, use me, and pour me out to touch other's lives."

---

13 Cited in David Brooks, "In Defense of Death," *New York Times,* January 12, 2009.

My favorite line in the movie *Chariots of Fire* occurred when Eric Liddell's sister Jenny tried to convince him not to run in an important race. He looked at her and said gently but with conviction, "Jenny, Jenny. God made me fast, and when I run, I feel his pleasure." Eric's perspective captures the essence of what it means to live wholeheartedly for Christ: God has given us talents and treasures, and when our love for God and for people prompts us to use them to touch lives, we sense the smile of God. That's enough of a reward for me, and it gives me a clear flight plan for every day of my life.

In this book, we've looked at many different tests God gives us, but they all point to a day when we receive our report card from Christ. If we grasp the significance of that moment, we'll be more passionate about following him, more thrilled to see him use us, and more hopeful that what we do each day makes a difference for all eternity.

Do you anticipate that day at the Judgment Seat with anxiety or joyful expectation? Explain your answer.

How are you doing right now on God's flight plan for your life?

What steps can you take as soon as you close this book that will cause your Creator and Savior to smile?

Jesus, when I stand before you on that day, I want...

ABOUT THE AUTHOR

Scott Wilson has been in full-time pastoral ministry for more than 20 years. He is the Senior Pastor of The Oaks Fellowship located in Dallas, Texas. In the last three years, the church has experienced robust growth, nearly tripling in size—now ministering to nearly 3000 people. The church currently offers five worship experiences on three different campuses to accommodate the growing crowds.

Scott is the CEO and founder of Scott Wilson Consulting; an organization that exists to come alongside church and marketplace leaders to enable them to achieve the full potential of what God has called them to do. Pastor Scott has a vision to strengthen and empower God's leaders to fulfill their destiny and dreams.

Scott and his father, Dr. Tom Wilson, lead one of the most innovative public school systems in the State of Texas. Life School currently educates over 3000 students in five locations in the Dallas area. Each year during open enrollment for new students, parents camp out overnight to enroll their children in these schools.

Under Scott's visionary leadership, The Oaks School of Leadership was founded in 1998. This school of ministry is in partnership with the Southwestern Assembly of God University in Waxahachie, Texas, and all students receive up to 48 university credit hours over a two-year period. They are eligible for grants and federal financial aide like any other major university. The primary purpose for The Oaks School of Leadership is to

train and equip the best leaders in the Kingdom of God and to be a leadership pipeline for the multi-site ministry of The Oaks and its partners around the world.

Finally, Scott is a loving husband and proud father. Scott and his wife, Jenni, have three boys: Dillon, Hunter, and Dakota. The Wilsons live in the Dallas area.

For more information concerning The Oaks Fellowship and their ministry resources, Scott Wilson Consulting, Life School, The Oaks School of Leadership, or to find a life coach, go to www.scottwilsonleadership.org.

USING *THE NEXT LEVEL* IN GROUPS AND CLASSES

This book is designed for individual study, small groups, and classes. The best way to absorb and apply these principles is for each person to individually study and answer the questions at the end of each chapter, then to discuss them in either a class or a group environment.

Each day's questions are designed to promote reflection, application, and discussion. Order enough copies of the book for everyone to have a copy. For couples, encourage both to have their own book so they can record their individual reflections.

A recommended schedule for a small group might be:

Week 1   Introduction to the material. The group leader can tell their own story, share their hopes for the group, and provide books for each person.

Weeks 2-6   If people in your group are going to use the book for 31 days in a row, you can lead discussions each week on Days 1-7, 8-14, 15-21, 22-28, and 29-31.

Or...

Weeks 2-7   If your group prefers to go through five lessons each week, you can lead discussions on Days 1-5, 6-10, 11-15, 16-20, 21-25, 26-31.

Or...

Weeks 2-11 You and your group may want to tackle only three days' lessons to discuss each week. If that's your plan, you may be able to have richer conversations about the ones you discuss each week.

Personalize Each Lesson

Don't feel pressured to cover every question in every lesson in your group discussions! Pick out one or two lessons that had the biggest impact on you, and focus on those, or ask people in the group to share their responses to the lessons that meant the most to them that week.

Make sure you personalize the principles and applications. At least once in each group meeting, add your own story to illustrate a particular point.

Make the Scriptures come alive. Far too often, we read the Bible like it's a phone book, with little or no emotion. Paint a vivid picture for people. Provide insights about the context of people's encounters with God, and help people in your class or group sense the emotions of specific people in each scene.

Focus on Application

The questions at the end of each chapter and your encouragement to be authentic will help your group take big steps to apply the principles they're learning. Share how you are applying the principles in particular chapters each week, and encourage them to take steps of growth, too.

Three Types of Questions

If you have led groups for a few years, you already understand the importance of using open questions to stimulate discussion. Three types of questions are limiting, leading, and open. Many of the questions at the end of each day's lessons are open questions.

- Limiting questions focus on an obvious answer, such as, "What does Jesus call himself in John 10:11?" These don't stimulate reflection or discussion. If you want to use questions like this, follow them with thought-provoking open questions.

- Leading questions sometimes require the listener to guess what the leader has in mind, such as, "Why did Jesus use the metaphor of a shepherd in John 10?" (He was probably alluding to a passage in Ezekiel, but most people wouldn't know that.) The teacher who asks a leading question has a definite answer in mind. Instead of asking this question, he should teach the point and perhaps ask an open question about the point he has made.

- Open questions usually don't have right or wrong answers. They stimulate thinking, and they are far less threatening because the person answering doesn't risk ridicule for being wrong. These questions often begin with "Why do you think...?" or "What are some reasons that...?" or "How would you have felt in that situation?"

Preparation

As you prepare to teach this material in a group or class, consider these steps:

1. Carefully and thoughtfully read the book. Make notes, highlight key sections, quotes, or stories, and complete the reflection sections at the end of each day's chapter. This will familiarize you with the entire scope of the content.

2. As you prepare for each week's class or group, read the corresponding chapters again and make additional notes.

3. Tailor the amount of content to the time allotted. You won't have time to cover all the questions, so pick the ones that are most pertinent.

4. Add your own stories to personalize the message and add impact.

5. Before and during your preparation, ask God to give you wisdom, clarity, and power. Trust Him to use your group to change people's lives.

6. Most people will get far more out of the group if they read the chapters and complete the reflection each week. Order books before the group or class begins or after the first week.

TO ORDER BOOKS AND OTHER RESOURCES

To order more copies of *The Next Level* and the Worship CD, go to:

www.journeytothenextlevel.com

For church leaders who want to know how to use *The Next Level* in their churches and their communities, go to:

www.nextlevelcampaign.com

A resource for church leaders:
Steering Through Chaos:
Mapping a clear direction in the midst of transition and change

This book provides leaders the insight, inspiration, and courage they need to anticipate change, prepare for transitions, and make the difficult choices that will keep their churches moving forward. Book and audio available in February 2010.

For more information, go to:

www.scottwilsonleadership.com